PRAIRIE STATE BOOKS

# Chicago Poems

# Carl Sandburg

# Chicago Poems

*Introduction by*
John E. Hallwas

UNIVERSITY OF ILLINOIS PRESS
*Urbana and Chicago*

Introduction © 1992 by the Board of Trustees
of the University of Illinois
Manufactured in the United States of America
P   5   4   3

*This book is printed on acid-free paper.*


Library of Congress Cataloging-in-Publication Data

Sandburg, Carl, 1878–1967.
 Chicago poems/Carl Sandburg; introduction by John E. Hallwas.
  p. cm.—(Prairie state books)
 Includes bibliographical references.
 ISBN 0-252-06234-5 (pb:alk. paper)
  1. Chicago (Ill.)—Poetry.   I. Hallwas, John E.   II. Title.
III. Series.
PS3537.A618C5   1992                              91-21284
811'.52—dc20                                         CIP

# Contents

## CONTENTS

## HANDFULS

# CONTENTS

# CONTENTS

# CONTENTS

## SHADOWS

## OTHER DAYS (1900–1910)

# Introduction

*John E. Hallwas*

*Chicago Poems* (1916) brought Carl Sandburg to national attention, and it remains one of the most widely known volumes of American poetry. A noted journalist, poet, folksong-singer, and biographer, Sandburg eventually became a much-celebrated and culturally significant figure. For most of the twentieth century he has symbolized our American myth of concern[1]—our civic belief in an inclusive, democratic social ideal—because of his rise from poverty, his poetry about the people, and his famous interpretation of Lincoln. Much about his life has become well known to the public, including the book that launched his literary career.

*Chicago Poems* also has an important place in American literary history. Published during the second decade of the century as part of the outpouring of "new poetry" that focused on the American experience, it followed such notable volumes as Robert Frost's *North of Boston* (1914), Vachel Lindsay's *The Congo and Other Poems* (1914), and Edgar Lee Masters's *Spoon River Anthology* (1915). Lindsay, Masters, and Sandburg became the main poets of the Chicago Renaissance, bringing midwestern poetry to national prominence for the first time. *Chicago Poems* was a tradition-shattering book, written in Whitmanesque free verse at a time when such poetic informalism was still controversial. But more importantly, it focused substantially on city life and expressed the poet's commitment to the masses. These two aspects are central to the continuing significance of *Chicago Poems*.

INTRODUCTION

Nothing about Sandburg's poetry is more important than his dis-
tinctive view of the poet's role. Deeply influenced by Whitman,
Sandburg rejected the concept of the isolated poet who creates art
out of a unique consciousness; instead, he viewed himself as a mod-
ern bard whose art was an extension of his culture. He wanted to be
"commensurate with a people"—as Whitman, in his preface to
*Leaves of Grass,* said the American bard must be.[2] Sandburg wanted
to help create a new cultural consciousness by reflecting and syn-
thesizing facets of the American experience in his time, especially
the spiritual condition of the people. That purpose is most obvious,
perhaps, in his book-length poem *The People, Yes* (1936), but it is
evident as well in *Chicago Poems, Cornhuskers* (1918), *Smoke and
Steel* (1920), *Slabs of the Sunburnt West* (1922), *Good Morning, Amer-
ica* (1928), and in some of his later poems. As Archibald MacLeish
said in a memorial tribute that later became his introduction to *The
Complete Poems of Carl Sandburg* (1970), "If ever a man wrote for a
particular people, however he may have reached in his heart for all
people, it was Sandburg."[3]

The term "bard" implies the celebration of a culture, especially
through recounting the deeds of heroes who embody the values of
their people, and that is the poet's oldest function. Perhaps the most
noted modern expression of that ancient literary purpose is Sand-
burg's massive Lincoln biography—a prose epic about the mythic
Great Emancipator, who embodied America's democratic ideal.
But for Sandburg, as for Whitman, the people themselves were a
kind of collective hero, and he celebrated them directly—as dream-
ing and struggling humankind in *The People, Yes* and as fragments of
the mass, representative American figures and groups, in many
shorter poems. Hence, *Chicago Poems* includes such works as "The
Shovel Man," "Ice Handler," "Muckers," and "Working Girls."
And as James Hurt has pointed out, in "Chicago" the city as a
whole is "a version of Sandburg's collective hero." Indeed, Chicago
is personified as a tough, confident young man, "bragging and
laughing that under his wrist is the pulse, and under his ribs is the
heart of the people."[4]

Sandburg's celebrative purpose in *Chicago Poems* is tempered by his equally forceful commitment to social criticism—a commitment that diminished substantially after the book was published. That aspect of his poetry resulted from his working-class background and socialist philosophy. His father, August Sandburg, worked ten hours a day, six days a week, with no vacations, as a "helper" in the Galesburg blacksmith shop of the Chicago, Burlington, and Quincy Railroad. He never complained about his long, hard days; nor was he a socialist. But being part of a laboring man's family made Carl naturally sympathetic to the socialist cause. And as a young man he held a variety of humble jobs, so he developed a deep sense of comradeship with those who toil and struggle and hope.

Sandburg's early years were marked by a succession of socialist influences. The first was a Mr. Sjodin, a Swedish tailor in Galesburg, who "was an anarchist, a Populist, and a Socialist, at home with anyone who was against the government and the plutocrats who rob the poor."[5] The tailor's son John held similar views and argued them so effectively that Sandburg, an admiring friend, remembered them half a century later. A more important influence was Philip Green Wright, a many-faceted professor at Galesburg's Lombard College, whose poems, such as "The Socialist" and "The Cry of the Underlings," express the desire for social change (although he apparently was not a socialist himself).[6] Wright encouraged Sandburg to write poetry, and his talented student did so with increasing capability. Sandburg also embraced socialism, which demanded radical change and fostered millennial hopes for a just and equitable society.

It is not surprising that Sandburg eventually became a lecturer and organizer for the Social Democratic party, which was emerging as an important political force, especially in Wisconsin. Sandburg moved there, started working for the cause, and soon met Lilian Steichen (whom he later called Paula). She was a committed socialist who characterized herself this way in a 1908 letter to Sandburg: "I don't go to church Sundays. . . . I talk socialism, and radicalism generally, whenever I get the chance."[7] Steichen encouraged her new comrade (and, later in 1908, her husband) to become "our Poet," the poet of the socialist movement, who would "add to the divine madness of poesy the diviner madness of revolutionary agitation."[8] During that same year Sandburg was involved in the presidential campaign of America's leading socialist, Eugene V. Debs, with whom he became acquainted. Two years later the young reporter and organizer worked for the Social Democratic campaign in Milwaukee, helping to elect Emil Seidel the first socialist mayor of an American city. For two years Sandburg was Mayor Seidel's private secretary, and he continued to lecture and write articles espousing the socialist cause.

Sandburg also continued to write poetry. As one might expect, the greatest challenge for him was to write poems that reflected the plight of lower-class Americans but did not become propaganda. Lyrics such as "Masses" and "I am the People, the Mob" reveal that he did not always succeed.

Sandburg's problem was similar to that of contemporary poet Carolyn Forché. A journalist and human rights investigator in El Salvador between 1978 and 1980, she subsequently turned to writing "a poetry of witness," identifying with those who struggle against oppressive social conditions. In an article for *The American Poetry Review*, Forché expresses the artistic problem of the politically engaged poet in terms that shed light on Sandburg's poetics: "All poetry is both pure and engaged, in the sense that it is made of language, but it is also art. Any theory which takes one half of the social-esthetic dynamic and accentuates it too much results in a breakdown. Stress of purity generates a feeble estheticism that fails, in its beauty, to communicate. On the other hand, propagandistic hack-work has no independent life as poetry. What matters is not whether a poem is political, but the quality of its engagement."[9] Forché also makes an important observation about the relationship between poetics and authority—that is, between poetry as an established art and the poet's reflection of experience: "From our tradition we inherit a poetic, a sense of appropriate subjects, styles, forms, and levels of diction," but "a poet's voice must be inwardly authentic and compelling of our attention; the poet's voice must have authority."[10] In short, significant poetry continually reflects the unpoetic, the "authenthic" experience from which the poet derives his or her authority. Through fidelity to the complexities of the actual, such poetry challenges the limits of what might be said, and in that sense it is inescapably political.

Sandburg did not write much about his poetics, but he clearly shared Forché's values and concerns. In his "Notes for a Preface" to *Complete Poems,* Sandburg refers to "poetry and politics, the relation of poets to society, to democracy, to monarchy, to dictatorships" as an important matter that is not well understood.[11] He also praises Stephen Vincent Benét as a poet of social consciousness, an advocate of freedom who " 'wrote often hoping that men would act because of his words.'" Sandburg undoubtedly thought of himself in that way too. After disparaging "formal poetry perfect only in form," he equates effective poetry with saying what must be said, expressing "the urge in the beginning."[12] That is, poets must not allow their authentic voices to be muffled by their art. As these comments suggest, decades before Forché, Sandburg was concerned about social responsibility and poetic authority. It is not surprising that he created an effective "poetry of witness"—to use Forché's term for poetry that is deeply engaged with the lives of the downtrodden and hence is politically sensitive.

In *Chicago Poems* Sandburg examines a level of American social experience that was not considered poetic. In fact, the title of the book is an oxymoron, for "Chicago" epitomized the harsh reality that was not reflected in "poems." But the lives of the poor, the laboring masses, which Sandburg understood so well from his experience as the son of a semiliterate railroad worker and his own work as a Social Democratic party organizer and urban journalist, constituted the foundation of his authority as a poet. Much of what "Chicago" stood for in the public mind was the very essence of his voice. Hence, in "The Right to Grief" he conveys his determination to bring the struggles and sorrows of America's desperately poor urban families into the public consciousness through his poetry. As the subtitle indicates, Sandburg addresses himself *"To Certain Poets About to Die"*—that is, to the tradition-bound poets of his time, who would find "the dead child of a stockyards hunky" beyond the limits of their poetic. In the poem itself he asserts his right to share the poor family's grief, and hence to bear witness to it, after he depicts the shocking reality of their response to the loss:

> The hunky and his wife and the kids
> Cry over the pinched face almost at peace in the white box.
> They remember it was scrawny and ran up high doctor bills.
> They are glad it is gone for the rest of the family now
>     will have more to eat and wear.
>
> Yet before the majesty of Death they cry around the coffin
> And wipe their eyes with red bandanas and sob when the
>     priest says, "God have mercy on us all."
>
> I have a right to feel my throat choke about this.
> You take your grief and I mine—see?

Sandburg's "right to grief" is not based simply on his empathy for the bereaved family but also stems from his recognition of what poverty has done to them. He is mourning not just the dead child but also the family's economic and spiritual condition. The poem is an act of social engagement, and it is inescapably political because it implies the failure of the American social ideal.

Mark Van Wienen points out that "*Chicago Poems* undermines the sharp opposition between poetry and politics, art and propaganda."[13] Because that is true, some of Sandburg's early critics had difficulty appreciating "political" poems like "The Right to Grief" and ascribed value only to the lyrics that do not reflect social conditions.[14] By doing so they badly misjudged the significance of the book, which is notable precisely because the poet so effectively conveys his social consciousness.

While writing the poems that appeared in the book Sandburg was well aware that he was challenging the established poetic. Indeed, a little-known poem called "Choices" makes that explicit. He asserts that he will not focus on the many well established, appro-

priate subjects for poetry but will concentrate on the harsh realities
that other poets omit:

> They offer you many things,
>     I a few.
> Moonlight on the play of fountains at night
> With water sparkling a drowsy monotone,
> Bare-shouldered, smiling women and talk
> And a cross-play of loves and adulteries
> And a fear of death
>                     and a remember of regrets:
> All this they offer you.
> I come with:
>     salt and bread
>     a terrible job of work
>     and tireless war;
> Come and have now:
>     hunger
>     danger
>     and hate.

Especially in the "Chicago Poems" section of the book, Sand-
burg strives to enact his daring new poetic that will not flinch at
hunger, danger, and hate—unpoetic realities of the human experi-
ence in urban-industrial America. Hence, his most famous poem,
"Chicago," affirms the evils of the city:

> They tell me you are wicked and I believe them, for I
>     have seen your painted women under the gas lamps
>     luring the farm boys.
> And they tell me you are crooked and I answer: Yes, it is
>     true I have seen the gunman kill and go free to kill
>     again.
> And they tell me you are brutal and my reply is: On the
>     faces of women and children I have seen the marks of
>     wanton hunger.

These lines have peculiar force because the poet is asserting his
role as witness: the city's reputation, its symbolic meaning as harsh

urban reality, is verified by experience ("I have seen"). Moreover, Sandburg is not a casual onlooker. He identifies with the human reality of Chicago; he is part of "this my city." He is not an isolated artist who can seek a personal resolution that distances him from the ugly aspects of his culture. Hence, he does not simply condemn the city, as so many writers before him did, including William T. Stead (*If Christ Came to Chicago* [1894]) and Upton Sinclair (*The Jungle* [1906]), two visitors who wrote best-selling exposés. Instead, Sandburg asserts his responsibility to his culture not only by witnessing the discouraging reality that he knows but by discerning those human forces that offer hope—the vitality, confidence, and determination of the people. Those forces in abundance are what make Chicago the "Hog Butcher, Tool Maker, Stacker of Wheat, Player with Railroads and Freight Handler to the Nation." The poem is not a defense of the city's evils but a refusal to see Chicago—or the urban-industrial society it symbolizes—from a partial or poetically idealized perspective. The city is an imperfect cultural hero, but a deeply American one.

"Chicago" is a mythic poem that invites the reader to identify with the city, to see urban-industrial society as the dynamic essence of America, where the people must work out their "terrible burden of destiny." The city is "cunning as a savage pitted against the wilderness" because urban people, immigrants and others, continue the struggle to establish America that is the core of our national experience. In the furious work of urban development, the "building, breaking, rebuilding" that forms the climax of the poem, lies the hope of finally establishing a society that is commensurate with our democratic myth of concern.

Most of the fifty-four poems that follow in the remarkable "Chicago Poems" section of the book portray facets of American urban-industrial life that must be evaluated in the context of that national ideal. For example, the workers in "Subway" who toil "Down between the walls of shadow / Where the iron laws insist" and the children in "They Will Say" who "work, broken and smothered, for bread and wages" contradict the American social ideal. They are victims. So is the frustrated speaker in "Blacklisted," who must give up his name to find work. But despite their oppressed situation the people struggle on with "the clutch of hope" in their faces, as the speaker notes in "Passers-by." Some even have occasional happy times, like the "crowd of Hungarians under the trees with their women and children and a keg of beer and an accordion," who are described by the poet-witness in "Happiness."

In a fine short article James Hurt views Sandburg's city poems as a commentary on "the American dream," a vague concept that, in his study, refers to our democratic myth of concern, "the Founders' dream" of an inclusive, equalitarian society, offering a better life for all:

> Sandburg's Chicago, built up of glimpses, vignettes, and fragmentary impressions, is a microcosm of turn-of-the-century America, confronting frightening new challenges to the American dream. There is grinding poverty, the remorseless struggle for existence that leads Mag's husband to cry, "I wish to God I never saw you, Mag." There are the injustices of class and ethnic prejudices, the gaps between rich and poor, native-born and immigrant, lucky and unlucky, which are summed up in "Child of the Romans," in the image of the dago shovelman sitting by the railroad track eating bread and bologna while a dining car whirls by full of people eating "steaks running with brown gravy, / Strawberries and cream, eclairs and coffee." And most of all, there is the growing standardization of man, a lowering of expectations, and a limited vision of possibility, summed up in "Limited" (a significant and ambiguous title) in the man who, asked where he is going, can imagine no answer to that question other than the "limited," literal one, "Omaha." [15]

Like the other socialists of his era, Sandburg felt that the democratic ideal was being subverted by a wealthy group that had established an economic system based on the exploitation of working-class people. The rich had perverted the American dream, changed

INTRODUCTION

it into a quest for wealth and social exclusivity. That is precisely
what is conveyed in the fine short poem called "A Fence":

> Now the stone house on the lake front is finished and
>     the workmen are beginning the fence.
> The palings are made of iron bars with steel points that
>     can stab the life out of any man who falls on them.
> As a fence, it is a masterpiece, and will shut off the
>     rabble and all vagabonds and hungry men and all
>     wandering children looking for a place to play.
> Passing through the bars and over the steel points will go
>     nothing except Death and the Rain and To-morrow.

To socialists the inordinate pursuit of private property by the well-
to-do caused inequality, lack of community, and eventual social dis-
ruption. That is what the fence around the lakefront mansion sym-
bolizes. The closing line of the poem suggests the inevitability of
social change, for a vicious barrier that causes resentment today is
apt to be penetrated "To-morrow."

Sandburg's commitment to socialism is evident in another way
as well: the men and women in *Chicago Poems* are essentially not
thinkers or lovers or family members but workers. The speaker in "I
am the People, the Mob" says, describing his collective self, "I am
the workingman, the inventor, the maker of the world's food and
clothes." The workers' honest labor, which contributes to society as
a whole, gives them dignity and makes them spiritually superior
to those who would exploit them. Hence, in "Onion Days" Mrs.
Pietro Giovannitti, who works ten to twelve hours a day picking
onions, is superior to her boss, Jasper, who sits in church and won-
ders how he can get more work for less money from his female la-
borers. Work is not usually a social evil, but it can be. Sandburg
portrays work as fulfilling when workers receive immediate personal
value from their efforts, as the fish crier does when he "dangles
herring before his prospective customers evincing a joy identical
with that of Pavlowa dancing." He is like the famous dancer be-
cause he is expressing himself through his work, fulfilling his poten-

tial. But Sandburg views work as spiritually destructive when it has no personal value, as in "Mill-Doors," where dehumanizing labor makes the exploited mill children old before they are young.

Sandburg wants the working people of America to be recognized as the builders and sustainers of our culture, as he indicates in "Ready to Kill." The speaker feels like smashing "a bronze memorial of a famous general / Riding horseback with a flag and a sword and a revolver on him" because it glorifies leaders who are "ready to kill anybody"—and "anybody" is always the people. Instead, the speaker wants memorials to "the farmer, the miner, the shop man, the factory hand, the fireman and the teamster." That is, he wants America to remember and celebrate its working people, and he will not be satisfied until some future day,

> When they stack a few silhouettes
> > Against the sky
> > Here in the park,
> And show the real huskies that are doing the work of the
> > world, and feeding people instead of butchering
> > them. . . .

As this imaginative smashing of the general's statue and erecting of memorials to the people reveals, Sandburg's poetry occasionally becomes symbolic action. It challenges what is and asserts what might be.

"Ready to Kill" reveals the importance of memory to the realization of America's democratic myth of concern, as do many other poems in the book. The pervasive theme of memory is, in fact, an aspect of the poet's role as witness: Sandburg wants his readers to remember the poor, the struggling masses. That is, if we are to approach the social ideal to which our nation is committed, we must remember the condition and the contribution of working-class Americans. Hence, the speaker in "Halsted Street Car" says to the cartoonists, who normally focus on the nation's leaders, "Find for your pencils / A way to mark your memory / Of tired empty faces"— the faces of those who work in the city. And in "I am the People, the

Mob" the collective speaker says, "I am the audience that witnesses history," but the downtrodden condition of the people continues because "I forget." A better day will come "when I, the People, learn to remember"—especially the struggles and betrayals of the past.

In "Skyscraper," which closes the "Chicago Poems" section, Sandburg asserts that America's myth of concern is still valid in twentieth-century urban-industrial society, and he places the contribution of workers at the center of our culture. He does so by viewing the skyscraper, that Chicago-born symbol of modern society, as a kind of monument to the working people who built it and occupy its offices:

> Men who sunk the pilings and mixed the mortar are laid
>     in graves where the wind whistles a wild song without
>     words
>
> And so are men who strung the wires and fixed the pipes and
>     tubes and those who saw it rise floor by floor.
>
> Souls of them all are here, even the hod carrier begging at
>     back doors hundreds of miles away and the bricklayer
>     who went to state's prison for shooting another man
>     while drunk.
> . . . . . . . . . . . . . . .
> Behind the signs on the doors they work and the walls tell
>     nothing from room to room.
>
> Ten-dollar-a-week stenographers take letters from
>     corporation officers, lawyers, efficiency
>     engineers. . . .
>
> Smiles and tears of each office girl go into the soul of
>     the building just the same as the master-men who rule
>     the building.

In a sense, the poem is an imaginative response to the poet-speaker's yearning, apparent in "Ready to Kill," for a suitable monument to the people. Indeed, the skyscraper symbolizes our democratic myth of concern. Anyone who works for it or within it is spiritually integrated with it: all workers are part of the social whole. Hence, through his symbolic skyscraper Sandburg asserts that our social ideal is still valid, still capable of unifying and directing the efforts of Americans, even in a modern urban-industrial setting.

The remaining parts of Sandburg's famous first book are not as impressive as the "Chicago Poems" section, but there are two other distinctive groups of related poems. One is "Shadows," which depicts the brutalizing impact of the city on women; the other is "War Poems (1914–1915)," which is composed of antiwar lyrics inspired by the outbreak of World War I.

The seven poems that comprise "Shadows" form a sequence that closes with "Gone," one of the most familiar and perhaps least understood of Sandburg's poems. The poem has been misinterpreted because it is often anthologized separately, and the sequence provides important clues to its meaning. Read by itself, "Gone" appears to describe an attractive young singer and dancer whose departure from the city saddens her admirers. However, the six preceding lyrics focus on urban prostitution. The first of these, "Poems Done on a Late Night Car," has three parts. In part 1 ("Chickens") the city speaks of its desire for "'girls fresh as country wild flowers, / With young faces tired of cows and barns'"; in part 2 ("Used Up") the mouths of prostitutes "beaten by the fists of / Men using them" are compared to "red roses, / Crushed"; and in part 3 ("Home") the speaker wishes that the world had more maternal love—which presumably would prevent the restlessness that causes young women to leave home for the city. Here too Sandburg asserts his role as witness: "Used Up" is subtitled *Lines based on certain regrets that come with rumination upon the painted faces of women on North Clark Street, Chicago.* In the second lyric, "It Is Much," the speaker advises streetwalkers, "women of night life," that "it is much to be warm and sure of to-morrow." That is, traditional home life is preferable to misdirected striving for self-fulfillment among the lights and shadows of the city at night. The next two poems are also about streetwalkers, and they vividly enlarge upon the "used up" theme of the opening lyric. "Trafficker" describes a prostitute with "beauty wasted, body faded, claims gone, / And no takers," while the female speaker in "Harrison Street Court" laments, "'I been hustlin' now / Till I ain't much good any more. / I got nothin' to show for it.'" The fifth and sixth poems depict prostitutes of a higher social class, both of whom were abandoned by men. The woman in "Soiled Dove" was "not a harlot until she married a corporation lawyer who picked her from a Ziegfield chorus"—and it was his infidelity that promoted her moral decline. In "Jungheimer's" a well-known saloon speaks, describing a painting within it—"of a woman half-dressed thrown reckless across a bed after a night of booze and riots." She is evidently a call girl abandoned by those who had hired her. The painting makes Jungheimer's a kind of continual witness to the social problem to which "Shadows" is devoted. It gives the otherwise typical saloon "a soul."

Chick Lorimer is undoubtedly also a prostitute. Her name connects her with the "Chickens" who are lured to the city in "Poems Done on a Late Night Car," and her singing and dancing evoke the harlot in "Soiled Dove." Hence, the opening line, "Everybody loved Chick Lorimer in our town," has a double meaning. But in one important respect she contrasts with the women in the six preceding poems: she is "a wild girl keeping a hold / On a dream she wants." Her life is focused, purposeful, irradiated by her dream. It is that which makes her fascinating—the girl "we all love." Indeed, it is that which makes her preeminently American. Soiled though she may be, Chick Lorimer is in the process of self-creation, and her pursuit of her dream allows her to transcend the circumstances that trap and destroy so many others. Thus, the important thing about Chick Lorimer is not "where she's gone" but the fact that she *is* gone—that her dream has redeemed her from what she has been. One of the finest poems in the volume, "Gone" is a stunning conclusion to a remarkable poetic sequence—and a testament to the redemptive power of dreams in a society where people are free to pursue them.

The "War Poems (1914–1915)" section reflects another aspect of Sandburg's role as witness. Perhaps the most interesting poem in this section is "Killers," in which the poet empathizes with soldiers that he does not actually see but cannot forget. His witnessing is based on heightened awareness:

> Under the sun
> Are sixteen million men,
> Chosen for shining teeth,
> Sharp eyes, hard legs,
> And a running of young warm blood in their wrists.
>
> And a red juice runs on the green grass;
> And a red juice soaks the dark soil.
> And the sixteen million are killing . . . and killing and
>     killing.
>
> I never forget them day or night:
> They'beat on my head for memory of them;
> They pound on my heart. . . .

Sandburg feels compelled to witness the killing, if only through imaginative identification with the soldiers, simply because of the war's enormity. He is obsessed by the massive, senseless slaughter, to the point where, as he says, "I wake in the night and smell the trenches."

Another example of imaginative witnessing is "Buttons." Like "Killers" it is an attempt to convey the human cost of World War I to a nation that was being drawn steadily closer to military involvement:

> I have been watching the war map slammed up for
>     advertising in front of the newspaper office.
> Buttons—red and yellow buttons—blue and black
>     buttons—are shoved back and forth across the map.
>
> A laughing young man, sunny with freckles,
> Climbs a ladder, yells a joke to somebody in the crowd,
> And then fixes a yellow button one inch west
> And follows the yellow button with a black button one inch
>     west.
>
> (Ten thousand men and boys twist on their bodies in a red
>     soak along a river edge,

<blockquote>
Gasping of wounds, calling for water, some rattling death
    in their throats.)
Who would guess what it cost to move two buttons one inch
    on the war map here in front of the newspaper office
    where the freckle-faced young man is laughing to us?
</blockquote>

"Buttons" is a poem about distance: the relationship between one inch on the map and the actual distance moved by the soldiers, measured by their agony; the physical distance that separates Americans from the Great War and makes a map necessary to convey what is happening; and the collapse of psychological distance between the poet-as-witness and the horrors of combat. It is an especially effective enactment of poetic empathy because the resistance to that response—the poet's distance from the war—is so fully realized.

Especially during the war, Sandburg wanted the American people to become more sensitive witnesses, and that involved promoting reflection as well as empathy. This aspect of his poetic purpose is conveyed in "Iron," where he describes "long, steel guns" on war ships, then "laughing lithe jackies [sailors]" who attend the guns, and finally, "broad, iron shovels" digging graves. Between the steel of the guns and the iron of the shovels are the sailors, "singing war songs, war chanties" and not fully realizing the peril of their situation. But Sandburg wants his readers to reflect on the inevitable relationship between war and graves, so he says, "I ask you / To witness— / The shovel is brother to the gun."

Two other antiwar poems convey the psychological impact of war on soldiers who have survived the fighting. The speaker in "Murmurings in a Field Hospital" is a wounded and spiritually shattered soldier who wants "no more iron cold and real to handle, / Shaped for a drive straight ahead." Instead he pleads, "Bring me only beautiful useless things. / Only old home things touched at sunset in the quiet." Like Hemingway's Nick Adams in "Big Two-Hearted River," he retreats into his uncomplicated, prewar past for psychological healing. And in "Fight" the speaker is perhaps in worse shape: he has been dehumanized by the killing. He enjoys it, so he feels the "red gluts and red hungers" in his bones and cries for war.

His experience has become his identity: "I was a killer. / Yes, I am a killer." These two poems are also a kind of witnessing through imaginative identification, and like so many other items in *Chicago Poems*, they break new poetic ground. They allow us to share the consciousness of the psychologically damaged.

The book has other successful poems, including two frequently anthologized imagistic pieces, "Fog" and "Nocturne in a Deserted Brickyard." But the significance of *Chicago Poems* surely resides in its challenge to the traditional poetic, its fierce engagement with aspects of the American experience that seemed inherently unpoetic. That Sandburg often lacked precision, that he failed to convey psychological complexity, and that his view of the people was uncritical are all undoubtedly true, but through his powerful poetry of witness he both advanced the social ideal to which America is committed and enlarged the poetic that he had inherited. Sandburg's early poems were inescapably political because his poetic voice was so deeply rooted in the experience of working-class Americans—the poor, the powerless, the victimized—the very people whose lives gave purpose to the socialist cause. But the best of those early poems are original and compelling. In the years that followed, Sandburg's love for America—and perhaps his socioeconomic rise— dissolved his critical perspective and eroded his poetic authority. He remained a sort of national bard, but he was no longer a fiercely engaged witness of the social reality that challenged our democratic myth of concern. Consequently, *Chicago Poems* is the apex of his poetic achievement.

## NOTES

1. Northrop Frye defines and discusses "myth of concern" in *The Critical Path* (Bloomington: Indiana University Press, 1971). As he points out, a myth of concern is a society's belief about itself, which encompasses its traditions, social duties, and ultimate destiny, and the function of such a myth is to hold a society together (p. 36). Frye also discusses "democracy" as a myth of concern, "an inclusive social ideal that works toward giving equal rights to all citizens" (p. 138). That Sandburg symbolized America's

INTRODUCTION

democratic myth of concern is apparent from the many books and articles that celebrate him as such a figure. In *The America of Carl Sandburg* (Washington, D.C.: University Press of Washington, D.C., 1965), for example, Hazel Durnell views him as a "symbol of America" who "articulates the social aims and aspirations" of his country (p. 214).

2. Walt Whitman, "Preface 1855—*Leaves of Grass*, First Edition," in *Leaves of Grass*, ed. Sculley Bradley and Harold W. Blodgett (New York: W. W. Norton, 1973), p. 713.

3. Archibald MacLeish, "Introduction," *The Complete Poems of Carl Sandburg* (New York: Harcourt, 1970), p. xx.

4. James Hurt, "Teaching Sandburg's *Chicago Poems*," *Illinois English Bulletin*, 69 (Winter 1982), 36.

5. Sandburg, *Always the Young Strangers* (New York: Harcourt, Brace, 1952), p. 206.

6. See Sandburg, *Ever the Winds of Chance* (Urbana: University of Illinois Press, 1983), p. 28.

7. Lilian Steichen to Carl Sandburg, March 7, 1908, in *The Poet and the Dream Girl: The Love Letters of Lilian Steichen and Carl Sandburg*, ed. Margaret Sandburg (Urbana: University of Illinois Press, 1987), p. 30.

8. Lilian Steichen to Carl Sandburg, February 24 and 29, 1908, in *The Poet and the Dream Girl*, pp. 16 and 21.

9. Carolyn Forché, "El Salvador: An Aide Memoir," *American Poetry Review*, July/August 1981, p. 6.

10. Ibid.

11. Sandburg, "Notes for a Preface," in *Complete Poems*, p. xxvi.

12. Ibid., p. xxvii.

13. Mark Van Wienen, "Taming the Socialist: Carl Sandburg's *Chicago Poems* and Its Critics," *American Literature*, 63 (1991), 99.

14. Van Wienen, pp. 94–96.

15. Hurt, pp. 37–38.

## SELECTED BIBLIOGRAPHY

Alexander, William. "The Limited American, the Great Loneliness, and the Singing Fire: Carl Sandburg's 'Chicago Poems,'" *American Literature*, 45 (1973–74), 67–83.

Allen, Gay Wilson. *Carl Sandburg*. University of Minnesota Pamphlets on American Writers, No. 101. Minneapolis: University of Minnesota Press, 1972.

# INTRODUCTION

Callahan, North. *Carl Sandburg: His Life and Works.* University Park: Pennsylvania State University Press, 1987.

Crowder, Richard. *Carl Sandburg.* New York: Twayne, 1964.

Duffey, Bernard. *The Chicago Renaissance in American Letters.* East Lansing: Michigan State University Press, 1954.

Durnell, Hazel. *The America of Carl Sandburg.* Washington, D.C.: University Press of Washington, D.C., 1965.

Golden, Harry. *Carl Sandburg.* 1961; Urbana: University of Illinois Press, 1988.

Hurt, James. "Teaching Sandburg's *Chicago Poems,*" *Illinois English Bulletin,* 69 (Winter 1982), 33–39.

Niven, Penelope. *Carl Sandburg: A Biography.* New York: Charles Scribner's Sons, 1991.

Rubin, Louis D., Jr. "Not to Forget Carl Sandburg . . . ," *Sewanee Review,* 85 (Winter 1977), 181–89.

Salwak, Dale. *Carl Sandburg: A Reference Guide.* Boston: G. K. Hall, 1988.

Sandburg, Carl. *The Complete Poems of Carl Sandburg.* New York: Harcourt Brace Jovanovich, 1970.

———. *The Letters of Carl Sandburg,* ed. Herbert Mitgang. New York: Harcourt, Brace and World, 1968.

Van Wienen, Mark. "Taming the Socialist: Carl Sandburg's *Chicago Poems* and Its Critics," *American Literature,* 63 (1991), 89–103.

# Chicago Poems

# CHICAGO

Hog Butcher for the World,
Tool Maker, Stacker of Wheat,
Player with Railroads and the Nation's Freight
Handler;
Stormy, husky, brawling,
City of the Big Shoulders:

They tell me you are wicked and I believe them, for I
have seen your painted women under the gas lamps
luring the farm boys.
And they tell me you are crooked and I answer: Yes, it
is true I have seen the gunman kill and go free to
kill again.
And they tell me you are brutal and my reply is: On the
faces of women and children I have seen the marks
of wanton hunger.
And having answered so I turn once more to those who
sneer at this my city, and I give them back the sneer
and say to them:
Come and show me another city with lifted head singing
so proud to be alive and coarse and strong and cun-
ning.
Flinging magnetic curses amid the toil of piling job on
job, here is a tall bold slugger set vivid against the
little soft cities;
Fierce as a dog with tongue lapping for action, cunning
as a savage pitted against the wilderness,
Bareheaded,
Shoveling,
Wrecking,
Planning,
Building, breaking, rebuilding,

Under the smoke, dust all over his mouth, laughing with
   white teeth,
Under the terrible burden of destiny laughing as a young
   man laughs,
Laughing even as an ignorant fighter laughs who has
   never lost a battle,
Bragging and laughing that under his wrist is the pulse,
   and under his ribs the heart of the people,
                      Laughing!
Laughing the stormy, husky, brawling laughter of
   Youth, half-naked, sweating, proud to be Hog
   Butcher, Tool Maker, Stacker of Wheat, Player with
   Railroads and Freight Handler to the Nation.

## SKETCH

THE shadows of the ships
Rock on the crest
In the low blue lustre
Of the tardy and the soft inrolling tide.

A long brown bar at the dip of the sky
Puts an arm of sand in the span of salt.

The lucid and endless wrinkles
Draw in, lapse and withdraw.
Wavelets crumble and white spent bubbles
Wash on the floor of the beach.

       Rocking on the crest
       In the low blue lustre
       Are the shadows of the ships.

## MASSES

Among the mountains I wandered and saw blue haze and
    red crag and was amazed;
On the beach where the long push under the endless tide
    maneuvers, I stood silent;
Under the stars on the prairie watching the Dipper slant
    over the horizon's grass, I was full of thoughts.
Great men, pageants of war and labor, soldiers and work-
    ers, mothers lifting their children—these all I
    touched, and felt the solemn thrill of them.
And then one day I got a true look at the Poor, millions
    of the Poor, patient and toiling; more patient than
    crags, tides, and stars; innumerable, patient as the
    darkness of night—and all broken, humble ruins of
    nations.

# LOST

DESOLATE and lone
All night long on the lake
Where fog trails and mist creeps,
The whistle of a boat
Calls and cries unendingly,
Like some lost child
In tears and trouble
Hunting the harbor's breast
And the harbor's eyes.

# THE HARBOR

Passing through huddled and ugly walls
By doorways where women
Looked from their hunger-deep eyes,
Haunted with shadows of hunger-hands,
Out from the huddled and ugly walls,
I came sudden, at the city's edge,
On a blue burst of lake,
Long lake waves breaking under the sun
On a spray-flung curve of shore;
And a fluttering storm of gulls,
Masses of great gray wings
And flying white bellies
Veering and wheeling free in the open.

# THEY WILL SAY

OF my city the worst that men will ever say is this:
You took little children away from the sun and the dew,
And the glimmers that played in the grass under the
    great sky,
And the reckless rain; you put them between walls
To work, broken and smothered, for bread and wages,
To eat dust in their throats and die empty-hearted
For a little handful of pay on a few Saturday nights.

# MILL-DOORS

You never come back.
I say good-by when I see you going in the doors,
The hopeless open doors that call and wait
And take you then for—how many cents a day?
How many cents for the sleepy eyes and fingers?

I say good-by because I know they tap your wrists,
In the dark, in the silence, day by day,
And all the blood of you drop by drop,
And you are old before you are young.
You never come back.

# HALSTED STREET CAR

Come you, cartoonists,
Hang on a strap with me here
At seven o'clock in the morning
On a Halsted street car.

Take your pencils
And draw these faces.

Try with your pencils for these crooked faces,
That pig-sticker in one corner—his mouth—
That overall factory girl—her loose cheeks.

Find for your pencils
A way to mark your memory
Of tired empty faces.

After their night's sleep,
In the moist dawn
And cool daybreak,
  Faces
Tired of wishes,
Empty of dreams.

# CLARK STREET BRIDGE

Dust of the feet
And dust of the wheels,
Wagons and people going,
All day feet and wheels.

Now.  .  .
.  .  Only stars and mist
A lonely policeman,
Two cabaret dancers,
Stars and mist again,
No more feet or wheels,
No more dust and wagons.

　　Voices of dollars
　　And drops of blood

　　.  .  .  .  .
　　Voices of broken hearts,
　　.  .  Voices singing, singing,
　　.  .  Silver voices, singing,
　　Softer than the stars,
　　Softer than the mist.

# PASSERS-BY

PASSERS-BY,
Out of your many faces
Flash memories to me
Now at the day end
Away from the sidewalks
Where your shoe soles traveled
And your voices rose and blent
To form the city's afternoon roar
Hindering an old silence.

Passers-by,
I remember lean ones among you,
Throats in the clutch of a hope,
Lips written over with strivings,
Mouths that kiss only for love,
Records of great wishes slept with,
    Held long
And prayed and toiled for:

    Yes,
Written on
Your mouths
And your throats
I read them
When you passed by.

# THE WALKING MAN OF RODIN

Legs hold a torso away from the earth.
And a regular high poem of legs is here.
Powers of bone and cord raise a belly and lungs
Out of ooze and over the loam where eyes look and ears
    hear
And arms have a chance to hammer and shoot and run
    motors.
            You make us
            Proud of our legs, old man.

And you left off the head here,
The skull found always crumbling neighbor of the
    ankles.

# SUBWAY

Down between the walls of shadow
Where the iron laws insist,
  The hunger voices mock.

The worn wayfaring men
With the hunched and humble shoulders,
  Throw their laughter into toil.

# THE SHOVEL MAN

On the street
Slung on his shoulder is a handle half way across,
Tied in a big knot on the scoop of cast iron
Are the overalls faded from sun and rain in the ditches;
Spatter of dry clay sticking yellow on his left sleeve
     And a flimsy shirt open at the throat,
     I know him for a shovel man,
     A dago working for a dollar six bits a day
And a dark-eyed woman in the old country dreams of
     him for one of the world's ready men with a pair
     of fresh lips and a kiss better than all the wild
     grapes that ever grew in Tuscany.

# A TEAMSTER'S FAREWELL

*Sobs En Route to a Penitentiary*

GOOD-BY now to the streets and the clash of wheels and
    locking hubs,
The sun coming on the brass buckles and harness knobs.
The muscles of the horses sliding under their heavy
    haunches,
Good-by now to the traffic policeman and his whistle,
The smash of the iron hoof on the stones,
All the crazy wonderful slamming roar of the street—
O God, there's noises I'm going to be hungry for.

# FISH CRIER

I KNOW a Jew fish crier down on Maxwell Street with a
  voice like a north wind blowing over corn stubble
  in January.
He dangles herring before prospective customers evinc-
  ing a joy identical with that of Pavlowa dancing.
His face is that of a man terribly glad to be selling fish,
  terribly glad that God made fish, and customers to
  whom he may call his wares from a pushcart.

# PICNIC BOAT

SUNDAY night and the park policemen tell each other it
    is dark as a stack of black cats on Lake Michigan.
A big picnic boat comes home to Chicago from the peach
    farms of Saugatuck.
Hundreds of electric bulbs break the night's darkness, a
    flock of red and yellow birds with wings at a stand-
    still.
Running along the deck railings are festoons and leap-
    ing in curves are loops of light from prow and stern
    to the tall smokestacks.
Over the hoarse crunch of waves at my pier comes a
    hoarse answer in the rhythmic oompa of the brasses
    playing a Polish folk-song for the home-comers.

## HAPPINESS

I ASKED professors who teach the meaning of life to tell
    me what is happiness.
And I went to famous executives who boss the work of
    thousands of men.
They all shook their heads and gave me a smile as though
    I was trying to fool with them.
And then one Sunday afternoon I wandered out along
    the Desplaines river
And I saw a crowd of Hungarians under the trees with
    their women and children and a keg of beer and an
    accordion.

# MUCKERS

TWENTY men stand watching the muckers.
  Stabbing the sides of the ditch
  Where clay gleams yellow,
  Driving the blades of their shovels
  Deeper and deeper for the new gas mains,
  Wiping sweat off their faces
    With red bandanas.
The muckers work on  .   .  pausing  .   .  to pull
Their boots out of suckholes where they slosh.


 Of the twenty looking on
Ten murmur, "O, it's a hell of a job,"
Ten others, "Jesus, I wish I had the job."

# BLACKLISTED

Why shall I keep the old name?
What is a name anywhere anyway?
A name is a cheap thing all fathers and mothers leave
each child:
A job is a job and I want to live, so
Why does God Almighty or anybody else care whether
I take a new name to go by?

# GRACELAND

Tomb of a millionaire,
A multi-millionaire, ladies and gentlemen,
Place of the dead where they spend every year
The usury of twenty-five thousand dollars
    For upkeep and flowers
To keep fresh the memory of the dead.
The merchant prince gone to dust
Commanded in his written will
Over the signed name of his last testament
Twenty-five thousand dollars be set aside
For roses, lilacs, hydrangeas, tulips,
For perfume and color, sweetness of remembrance
Around his last long home.

(A hundred cash girls want nickels to go to the movies
    to-night.
In the back stalls of a hundred saloons, women are at
    tables
Drinking with men or waiting for men jingling loose
    silver dollars in their pockets.
In a hundred furnished rooms is a girl who sells silk or
    dress goods or leather stuff for six dollars a week
    wages
And when she pulls on her stockings in the morning she
    is reckless about God and the newspapers and the
    police, the talk of her home town or the name
    people call her.)

# CHILD OF THE ROMANS

THE dago shovelman sits by the railroad track
Eating a noon meal of bread and bologna.
    A train whirls by, and men and women at tables
    Alive with red roses and yellow jonquils,
    Eat steaks running with brown gravy,
    Strawberries and cream, eclaires and coffee.
The dago shovelman finishes the dry bread and bologna,
Washes it down with a dipper from the water-boy,
And goes back to the second half of a ten-hour day's
    work
Keeping the road-bed so the roses and jonquils
Shake hardly at all in the cut glass vases
Standing slender on the tables in the dining cars.

# THE RIGHT TO GRIEF

*To Certain Poets About to Die*

TAKE your fill of intimate remorse, perfumed sorrow,
Over the dead child of a millionaire,
And the pity of Death refusing any check on the bank
Which the millionaire might order his secretary to
    scratch off
And get cashed.

  Very well,
You for your grief and I for mine.
Let me have a sorrow my own if I want to.

I shall cry over the dead child of a stockyards hunky.
His job is sweeping blood off the floor.
He gets a dollar seventy cents a day when he works
And it's many tubs of blood he shoves out with a broom
    day by day.

Now his three year old daughter
Is in a white coffin that cost him a week's wages.
Every Saturday night he will pay the undertaker fifty
    cents till the debt is wiped out.

The hunky and his wife and the kids
Cry over the pinched face almost at peace in the white
    box.

They remember it was scrawny and ran up high doctor
    bills.
They are glad it is gone for the rest of the family now
    will have more to eat and wear.

Yet before the majesty of Death they cry around the coffin

And wipe their eyes with red bandanas and sob when the priest says, " God have mercy on us all."

I have a right to feel my throat choke about this.

You take your grief and I mine—see?

To-morrow there is no funeral and the hunky goes back to his job sweeping blood off the floor at a dollar seventy cents a day.

All he does all day long is keep on shoving hog blood ahead of him with a broom.

# MAG

I WISH to God I never saw you, Mag.

I wish you never quit your job and came along with me.

I wish we never bought a license and a white dress

For you to get married in the day we ran off to a minister

And told him we would love each other and take care of each other

Always and always long as the sun and the rain lasts anywhere.

Yes, I'm wishing now you lived somewhere away from here

And I was a bum on the bumpers a thousand miles away dead broke.

    I wish the kids had never come

    And rent and coal and clothes to pay for

    And a grocery man calling for cash,

    Every day cash for beans and prunes.

    I wish to God I never saw you, Mag.

    I wish to God the kids had never come.

# ONION DAYS

MRS. GABRIELLE GIOVANNITTI comes along Peoria Street
  every morning at nine o'clock
With kindling wood piled on top of her head, her eyes
  looking straight ahead to find the way for her old
  feet.
Her daughter-in-law, Mrs. Pietro Giovannitti, whose
  husband was killed in a tunnel explosion through
  the negligence of a fellow-servant,
Works ten hours a day, sometimes twelve, picking onions
  for Jasper on the Bowmanville road.
She takes a street car at half-past five in the morning,
  Mrs. Pietro Giovannitti does,
And gets back from Jasper's with cash for her day's
  work, between nine and ten o'clock at night.
Last week she got eight cents a box, Mrs. Pietro Gio-
  vannitti, picking onions for Jasper,
But this week Jasper dropped the pay to six cents a
  box because so many women and girls were answer-
  ing the ads in the *Daily News*.
Jasper belongs to an Episcopal church in Ravenswood
  and on certain Sundays
He enjoys chanting the Nicene creed with his daughters
  on each side of him joining their voices with his.
If the preacher repeats old sermons of a Sunday, Jas-
  per's mind wanders to his 700-acre farm and how he
  can make it produce more efficiently
And sometimes he speculates on whether he could word
  an ad in the *Daily News* so it would bring more
  women and girls out to his farm and reduce operat-
  ing costs.

Mrs. Pietro Giovannitti is far from desperate about life;
   her joy is in a child she knows will arrive to her in
   three months.
And now while these are the pictures for today there are
   other pictures of the Giovannitti people I could give
   you for to-morrow,
And how some of them go to the county agent on win-
   ter mornings with their baskets for beans and corn-
   meal and molasses.
I listen to fellows saying here's good stuff for a novel or
   it might be worked up into a good play.
I say there's no dramatist living can put old Mrs.
   Gabrielle Giovannitti into a play with that kindling
   wood piled on top of her head coming along Peoria
   Street nine o'clock in the morning.

## POPULATION DRIFTS

NEW-MOWN hay smell and wind of the plain made her
a woman whose ribs had the power of the hills in
them and her hands were tough for work and there
was passion for life in her womb.

She and her man crossed the ocean and the years that
marked their faces saw them haggling with landlords
and grocers while six children played on the stones
and prowled in the garbage cans.

One child coughed its lungs away, two more have ade-
noids and can neither talk nor run like their mother,
one is in jail, two have jobs in a box factory

And as they fold the pasteboard, they wonder what the
wishing is and the wistful glory in them that flut-
ters faintly when the glimmer of spring comes on
the air or the green of summer turns brown:

They do not know it is the new-mown hay smell calling
and the wind of the plain praying for them to come
back and take hold of life again with tough hands
and with passion.

# CRIPPLE

ONCE when I saw a cripple
Gasping slowly his last days with the white plague,
Looking from hollow eyes, calling for air,
Desperately gesturing with wasted hands
In the dark and dust of a house down in a slum,
I said to myself
I would rather have been a tall sunflower
Living in a country garden
Lifting a golden-brown face to the summer,
Rain-washed and dew-misted,
Mixed with the poppies and ranking hollyhocks,
And wonderingly watching night after night
The clear silent processionals of stars.

## A FENCE

Now the stone house on the lake front is finished and the
      workmen are beginning the fence.
The palings are made of iron bars with steel points that
      can stab the life out of any man who falls on them.
As a fence, it is a masterpiece, and will shut off the rab-
      ble and all vagabonds and hungry men and all wan-
      dering children looking for a place to play.
Passing through the bars and over the steel points will go
      nothing except Death and the Rain and To-morrow.

# ANNA IMROTH

CROSS the hands over the breast here—so.
Straighten the legs a little more—so.
And call for the wagon to come and take her home.
Her mother will cry some and so will her sisters and
brothers.
But all of the others got down and they are safe and
this is the only one of the factory girls who
wasn't lucky in making the jump when the fire
broke.
It is the hand of God and the lack of fire escapes.

# WORKING GIRLS

THE working girls in the morning are going to work—
long lines of them afoot amid the downtown stores
and factories, thousands with little brick-shaped
lunches wrapped in newspapers under their arms.

Each morning as I move through this river of young-
woman life I feel a wonder about where it is all
going, so many with a peach bloom of young years
on them and laughter of red lips and memories in
their eyes of dances the night before and plays and
walks.

Green and gray streams run side by side in a river and
so here are always the others, those who have been
over the way, the women who know each one the
end of life's gamble for her, the meaning and the
clew, the how and the why of the dances and the
arms that passed around their waists and the fingers
that played in their hair.

Faces go by written over: " I know it all, I know where
the bloom and the laughter go and I have memo-
ries," and the feet of these move slower and they
have wisdom where the others have beauty.

So the green and the gray move in the early morning
on the downtown streets.

# MAMIE

MAMIE beat her head against the bars of a little Indiana town and dreamed of romance and big things off somewhere the way the railroad trains all ran.

She could see the smoke of the engines get lost down where the streaks of steel flashed in the sun and when the newspapers came in on the morning mail she knew there was a big Chicago far off, where all the trains ran.

She got tired of the barber shop boys and the post office chatter and the church gossip and the old pieces the band played on the Fourth of July and Decoration Day

And sobbed at her fate and beat her head against the bars and was going to kill herself

When the thought came to her that if she was going to die she might as well die struggling for a clutch of romance among the streets of Chicago.

She has a job now at six dollars a week in the basement of the Boston Store

And even now she beats her head against the bars in the same old way and wonders if there is a bigger place the railroads run to from Chicago where maybe there is

> romance
> and big things
> and real dreams
> that never go smash.

# PERSONALITY

*Musings of a Police Reporter in the Identification Bureau*

You have loved forty women, but you have only one thumb.

You have led a hundred secret lives, but you mark only one thumb.

You go round the world and fight in a thousand wars and win all the world's honors, but when you come back home the print of the one thumb your mother gave you is the same print of thumb you had in the old home when your mother kissed you and said good-by.

Out of the whirling womb of time come millions of men and their feet crowd the earth and they cut one anothers' throats for room to stand and among them all are not two thumbs alike.

Somewhere is a Great God of Thumbs who can tell the inside story of this.

# CUMULATIVES

STORMS have beaten on this point of land
And ships gone to wreck here
      and the passers-by remember it
      with talk on the deck at night
      as they near it.

Fists have beaten on the face of this old prize-fighter
And his battles have held the sporting pages
      and on the street they indicate him with their
      right fore-finger as one who once wore
      a championship belt.

A hundred stories have been published and a thousand
    rumored
About why this tall dark man has divorced two beau-
    tiful young women
And married a third who resembles the first two
      and they shake their heads and say, " There he
        goes,"
      when he passes by in sunny weather or in rain
      along the city streets.

## TO CERTAIN JOURNEYMEN

UNDERTAKERS, hearse drivers, grave diggers,
I speak to you as one not afraid of your business.

You handle dust going to a long country,
You know the secret behind your job is the same whether
  you lower the coffin with modern, automatic ma-
  chinery, well-oiled and noiseless, or whether the
  body is laid in by naked hands and then covered
  by the shovels.

Your day's work is done with laughter many days of the
  year,
And you earn a living by those who say good-by today
  in thin whispers.

# CHAMFORT

There's Chamfort. He's a sample.
Locked himself in his library with a gun,
Shot off his nose and shot out his right eye.
And this Chamfort knew how to write
And thousands read his books on how to live,
But he himself didn't know
How to die by force of his own hand—see?
They found him a red pool on the carpet
Cool as an April forenoon,
Talking and talking gay maxims and grim epi-
    grams.
Well, he wore bandages over his nose and right
    eye,
Drank coffee and chatted many years
With men and women who loved him
Because he laughed and daily dared Death:
" Come and take me."

## LIMITED

I AM riding on a limited express, one of the crack trains of the nation.

Hurtling across the prairie into blue haze and dark air go fifteen all-steel coaches holding a thousand people.

(All the coaches shall be scrap and rust and all the men and women laughing in the diners and sleepers shall pass to ashes.)

I ask a man in the smoker where he is going and he answers: " Omaha."

# THE HAS-BEEN

A STONE face higher than six horses stood five thousand
   years gazing at the world seeming to clutch a secret.
A boy passes and throws a niggerhead that chips off the
   end of the nose from the stone face; he lets fly a
   mud ball that spatters the right eye and cheek of the
   old looker-on.
The boy laughs and goes whistling " ee-ee-ee ee-ee-ee."
   The stone face stands silent, seeming to clutch a
   secret.

# A COIN

YOUR western heads here cast on money,
You are the two that fade away together,
    Partners in the mist.

    Lunging buffalo shoulder,
    Lean Indian face,
We who come after where you are gone
Salute your forms on the new nickel.

    You are
    To us:
    The past.

    Runners
    On the prairie:
    Good-by.

# DYNAMITER

I SAT with a dynamiter at supper in a German saloon
  eating steak and onions.

And he laughed and told stories of his wife and children
  and the cause of labor and the working class.

It was laughter of an unshakable man knowing life to be
  a rich and red-blooded thing.

Yes, his laugh rang like the call of gray birds filled with
  a glory of joy ramming their winged flight through
  a rain storm.

His name was in many newspapers as an enemy of the
  nation and few keepers of churches or schools would
  open their doors to him.

Over the steak and onions not a word was said of his
  deep days and nights as a dynamiter.

Only I always remember him as a lover of life, a lover
  of children, a lover of all free, reckless laughter
  everywhere—lover of red hearts and red blood the
  world over.

## ICE HANDLER

I KNOW an ice handler who wears a flannel shirt with
    pearl buttons the size of a dollar,
And he lugs a hundred-pound hunk into a saloon ice-
    box, helps himself to cold ham and rye bread,
Tells the bartender it's hotter than yesterday and will be
    hotter yet to-morrow, by Jesus,
And is on his way with his head in the air and a hard
    pair of fists.
He spends a dollar or so every Saturday night on a two
    hundred pound woman who washes dishes in the
    Hotel Morrison.
He remembers when the union was organized he broke
    the noses of two scabs and loosened the nuts so the
    wheels came off six different wagons one morning,
    and he came around and watched the ice melt in the
    street.
All he was sorry for was one of the scabs bit him on the
    knuckles of the right hand so they bled when he
    came around to the saloon to tell the boys about it.

# JACK

JACK was a swarthy, swaggering son-of-a-gun.

He worked thirty years on the railroad, ten hours a day, and his hands were tougher than sole leather.

He married a tough woman and they had eight children and the woman died and the children grew up and went away and wrote the old man every two years.

He died in the poorhouse sitting on a bench in the sun telling reminiscences to other old men whose women were dead and children scattered.

There was joy on his face when he died as there was joy on his face when he lived—he was a swarthy, swaggering son-of-a-gun.

# FELLOW CITIZENS

I DRANK musty ale at the Illinois Athletic Club with
the millionaire manufacturer of Green River butter
one night
And his face had the shining light of an old-time Quaker,
he spoke of a beautiful daughter, and I knew he had
a peace and a happiness up his sleeve somewhere.
Then I heard Jim Kirch make a speech to the Advertis-
ing Association on the trade resources of South
America.
And the way he lighted a three-for-a-nickel stogie and
cocked it at an angle regardless of the manners of
our best people,
I knew he had a clutch on a real happiness even though
some of the reporters on his newspaper say he is
the living double of Jack London's Sea Wolf.
In the mayor's office the mayor himself told me he was
happy though it is a hard job to satisfy all the office-
seekers and eat all the dinners he is asked to eat.
Down in Gilpin Place, near Hull House, was a man with
his jaw wrapped for a bad toothache,
And he had it all over the butter millionaire, Jim Kirch
and the mayor when it came to happiness.
He is a maker of accordions and guitars and not only
makes them from start to finish, but plays them
after he makes them.
And he had a guitar of mahogany with a walnut bottom
he offered for seven dollars and a half if I wanted it,
And another just like it, only smaller, for six dollars,
though he never mentioned the price till I asked
him,

And he stated the price in a sorry way, as though the
music and the make of an instrument count for a
million times more than the price in money.

I thought he had a real soul and knew a lot about God.

There was light in his eyes of one who has conquered
sorrow in so far as sorrow is conquerable or worth
conquering.

Anyway he is the only Chicago citizen I was jealous of
that day.

He played a dance they play in some parts of Italy
when the harvest of grapes is over and the wine
presses are ready for work.

# NIGGER

I AM the nigger.
Singer of songs,
Dancer. . .
Softer than fluff of cotton. . .
Harder than dark earth
Roads beaten in the sun
By the bare feet of slaves. . .
Foam of teeth . . . breaking crash of laughter. . .
Red love of the blood of woman,
White love of the tumbling pickaninnies. . .
Lazy love of the banjo thrum. . .
Sweated and driven for the harvest-wage,
Loud laugher with hands like hams,
Fists toughened on the handles,
Smiling the slumber dreams of old jungles,
Crazy as the sun and dew and dripping, heaving life
    of the jungle,
Brooding and muttering with memories of shackles:
                I am the nigger.
                Look at me.
                I am the nigger.

# TWO NEIGHBORS

FACES of two eternities keep looking at me.
One is Omar Khayam and the red stuff
    wherein men forget yesterday and to-morrow
    and remember only the voices and songs,
    the stories, newspapers and fights of today.
One is Louis Cornaro and a slim trick
    of slow, short meals across slow, short years,
    letting Death open the door only in slow, short
        inches.
I have a neighbor who swears by Omar.
I have a neighbor who swears by Cornaro.
                    Both are happy.
Faces of two eternities keep looking at me.
                    Let them look.

# STYLE

STYLE—go ahead talking about style.
You can tell where a man gets his style just
    as you can tell where Pavlowa got her legs
    or Ty Cobb his batting eye.

    Go on talking.
Only don't take my style away.
    It's my face.
    Maybe no good
        but anyway, my face.
I talk with it, I sing with it, I see, taste and feel with it,
    I know why I want to keep it.

Kill my style
        and you break Pavlowa's legs,
        and you blind Ty Cobb's batting eye.

# TO BEACHEY, 1912

Riding against the east,
A veering, steady shadow
Purrs the motor-call
Of the man-bird
Ready with the death-laughter
In his throat
And in his heart always
The love of the big blue beyond.

Only a man,
A far fleck of shadow on the east
Sitting at ease
With his hands on a wheel
And around him the large gray wings.
Hold him, great soft wings,
Keep and deal kindly, O wings,
With the cool, calm shadow at the wheel.

## UNDER A HAT RIM

WHILE the hum and the hurry
Of passing footfalls
Beat in my ear like the restless surf
Of a wind-blown sea,
A soul came to me
Out of the look on a face.

Eyes like a lake
Where a storm-wind roams
Caught me from under
The rim of a hat.
     I thought of a midsea wreck
     and bruised fingers clinging
     to a broken state-room door.

# IN A BREATH

*To the Williamson Brothers*

HIGH noon. White sun flashes on the Michigan Avenue
asphalt. Drum of hoofs and whirr of motors.
Women trapsing along in flimsy clothes catching
play of sun-fire to their skin and eyes.

Inside the playhouse are movies from under the sea.
From the heat of pavements and the dust of side-
walks, passers-by go in a breath to be witnesses of
large cool sponges, large cool fishes, large cool val-
leys and ridges of coral spread silent in the soak of
the ocean floor thousands of years.

A naked swimmer dives. A knife in his right hand
shoots a streak at the throat of a shark. The tail
of the shark lashes. One swing would kill the swim-
mer. . . Soon the knife goes into the soft under-
neck of the veering fish. . . Its mouthful of teeth,
each tooth a dagger itself, set row on row, glistens
when the shuddering, yawning cadaver is hauled up
by the brothers of the swimmer.

Outside in the street is the murmur and singing of life
in the sun—horses, motors, women trapsing along
in flimsy clothes, play of sun-fire in their blood.

# BATH

A MAN saw the whole world as a grinning skull and cross-bones. The rose flesh of life shriveled from all faces. Nothing counts. Everything is a fake. Dust to dust and ashes to ashes and then an old darkness and a useless silence. So he saw it all. Then he went to a Mischa Elman concert. Two hours waves of sound beat on his eardrums. Music washed something or other inside him. Music broke down and rebuilt something or other in his head and heart. He joined in five encores for the young Russian Jew with the fiddle. When he got outside his heels hit the sidewalk a new way. He was the same man in the same world as before. Only there was a singing fire and a climb of roses everlastingly over the world he looked on.

# BRONZES

THE bronze General Grant riding a bronze horse in Lincoln Park
Shrivels in the sun by day when the motor cars whirr by in long processions going somewhere to keep appointment for dinner and matineés and buying and selling
Though in the dusk and nightfall when high waves are piling
On the slabs of the promenade along the lake shore near by
I have seen the general dare the combers come closer
And make to ride his bronze horse out into the hoofs and guns of the storm.

I cross Lincoln Park on a winter night when the snow
  is falling.
Lincoln in bronze stands among the white lines of snow,
  his bronze forehead meeting soft echoes of the new-
  sies crying forty thousand men are dead along the
  Yser, his bronze ears listening to the mumbled roar
  of the city at his bronze feet.
A lithe Indian on a bronze pony, Shakespeare seated with
  long legs in bronze, Garibaldi in a bronze cape, they
  hold places in the cold, lonely snow to-night on their
  pedestals and so they will hold them past midnight
  and into the dawn.

# DUNES

WHAT do we see here in the sand dunes of the white
   moon alone with our thoughts, Bill,
Alone with our dreams, Bill, soft as the women tying
   scarves around their heads dancing,
Alone with a picture and a picture coming one after the
   other of all the dead,
The dead more than all these grains of sand one by one
   piled here in the moon,
Piled against the sky-line taking shapes like the hand of
   the wind wanted,
What do we see here, Bill, outside of what the wise men
   beat their heads on,
Outside of what the poets cry for and the soldiers drive
   on headlong and leave their skulls in the sun for—
   what, Bill?

## ON THE WAY

LITTLE one, you have been buzzing in the books,
Flittering in the newspapers and drinking beer with
    lawyers
And amid the educated men of the clubs you have been
    getting an earful of speech from trained tongues.
Take an earful from me once, go with me on a hike
Along sand stretches on the great inland sea here
And while the eastern breeze blows on us and the rest-
    less surge
Of the lake waves on the breakwater breaks with an ever
    fresh monotone,
Let us ask ourselves: What is truth? what do you or I
    know?
How much do the wisest of the world's men know about
    where the massed human procession is going?

You have heard the mob laughed at?
I ask you: Is not the mob rough as the mountains are
    rough?
And all things human rise from the mob and relapse and
    rise again as rain to the sea?

# READY TO KILL

TEN minutes now I have been looking at this.
I have gone by here before and wondered about it.
This is a bronze memorial of a famous general
Riding horseback with a flag and a sword and a revolver
     on him.
I want to smash the whole thing into a pile of junk to be
     hauled away to the scrap yard.
I put it straight to you,
After the farmer, the miner, the shop man, the factory
     hand, the fireman and the teamster,
Have all been remembered with bronze memorials,
Shaping them on the job of getting all of us
Something to eat and something to wear,
When they stack a few silhouettes
          Against the sky
          Here in the park,
And show the real huskies that are doing the work of
     the world, and feeding people instead of butchering
     them,
Then maybe I will stand here
And look easy at this general of the army holding a flag
     in the air,
And riding like hell on horseback
Ready to kill anybody that gets in his way,
Ready to run the red blood and slush the bowels of men
     all over the sweet new grass of the prairie.

# TO A CONTEMPORARY BUNKSHOOTER

You come along. . . tearing your shirt. . . yelling about
   Jesus.
   Where do you get that stuff?
   What do you know about Jesus?
Jesus had a way of talking soft and outside of a few
   bankers and higher-ups among the con men of Jeru-
   salem everybody liked to have this Jesus around be-
   cause he never made any fake passes and everything
   he said went and he helped the sick and gave the
   people hope.


You come along squirting words at us, shaking your fist
   and calling us all dam fools so fierce the froth slob-
   bers over your lips. . . always blabbing we're all
   going to hell straight off and you know all about it.


I've read Jesus' words. I know what he said. You don't
   throw any scare into me. I've got your number. I
   know how much you know about Jesus.
He never came near clean people or dirty people but
   they felt cleaner because he came along. It was your
   crowd of bankers and business men and lawyers
   hired the sluggers and murderers who put Jesus out
   of the running.


I say the same bunch backing you nailed the nails into
   the hands of this Jesus of Nazareth. He had lined
   up against him the same crooks and strong-arm men
   now lined up with you paying your way.

This Jesus was good to look at, smelled good, listened good. He threw out something fresh and beautiful from the skin of his body and the touch of his hands wherever he passed along.

You slimy bunkshooter, you put a smut on every human blossom in reach of your rotten breath belching about hell-fire and hiccupping about this Man who lived a clean life in Galilee.

When are you going to quit making the carpenters build emergency hospitals for women and girls driven crazy with wrecked nerves from your gibberish about Jesus—I put it to you again: Where do you get that stuff; what do you know about Jesus?

Go ahead and bust all the chairs you want to. Smash a whole wagon load of furniture at every performance. Turn sixty somersaults and stand on your nutty head. If it wasn't for the way you scare the women and kids I'd feel sorry for you and pass the hat.

I like to watch a good four-flusher work, but not when he starts people puking and calling for the doctors.

I like a man that's got nerve and can pull off a great original performance, but you—you're only a bughouse peddler of second-hand gospel—you're only shoving out a phoney imitation of the goods this Jesus wanted free as air and sunlight.

You tell people living in shanties Jesus is going to fix it up all right with them by giving them mansions in the skies after they're dead and the worms have eaten 'em.

You tell $6 a week department store girls all they need is Jesus; you take a steel trust wop, dead without having lived, gray and shrunken at forty years of age, and you tell him to look at Jesus on the cross and he'll be all right.

You tell poor people they don't need any more money on pay day and even if it's fierce to be out of a job, Jesus'll fix that up all right, all right—all they gotta do is take Jesus the way you say.

I'm telling you Jesus wouldn't stand for the stuff you're handing out. Jesus played it different. The bankers and lawyers of Jerusalem got their sluggers and murderers to go after Jesus just because Jesus wouldn't play their game. He didn't sit in with the big thieves.

I don't want a lot of gab from a bunkshooter in my religion.

I won't take my religion from any man who never works except with his mouth and never cherishes any memory except the face of the woman on the American silver dollar.

I ask you to come through and show me where you're pouring out the blood of your life.

I've been to this suburb of Jerusalem they call Golgotha,
where they nailed Him, and I know if the story is
straight it was real blood ran from His hands and
the nail-holes, and it was real blood spurted in red
drops where the spear of the Roman soldier rammed
in between the ribs of this Jesus of Nazareth.

# SKYSCRAPER

By day the skyscraper looms in the smoke and sun and
  has a soul.
Prairie and valley, streets of the city, pour people into
  it and they mingle among its twenty floors and are
  poured out again back to the streets, prairies and
  valleys.
It is the men and women, boys and girls so poured in and
  out all day that give the building a soul of dreams
  and thoughts and memories.
(Dumped in the sea or fixed in a desert, who would care
  for the building or speak its name or ask a police-
  man the way to it?)

Elevators slide on their cables and tubes catch letters and
  parcels and iron pipes carry gas and water in and
  sewage out.
Wires climb with secrets, carry light and carry words,
  and tell terrors and profits and loves—curses of men
  grappling plans of business and questions of women
  in plots of love.

Hour by hour the caissons reach down to the rock of the
  earth and hold the building to a turning planet.
Hour by hour the girders play as ribs and reach out and
  hold together the stone walls and floors.
Hour by hour the hand of the mason and the stuff of the
  mortar clinch the pieces and parts to the shape an
  architect voted.
Hour by hour the sun and the rain, the air and the rust,
  and the press of time running into centuries, play
  on the building inside and out and use it.

Men who sunk the pilings and mixed the mortar are laid
in graves where the wind whistles a wild song with-
out words

And so are men who strung the wires and fixed the pipes
and tubes and those who saw it rise floor by floor.

Souls of them all are here, even the hod carrier begging
at back doors hundreds of miles away and the brick-
layer who went to state's prison for shooting another
man while drunk.

(One man fell from a girder and broke his neck at the
end of a straight plunge—he is here—his soul has
gone into the stones of the building.)

On the office doors from tier to tier—hundreds of names
and each name standing for a face written across
with a dead child, a passionate lover, a driving am-
bition for a million dollar business or a lobster's
ease of life.

Behind the signs on the doors they work and the walls
tell nothing from room to room.

Ten-dollar-a-week stenographers take letters from cor-
poration officers, lawyers, efficiency engineers, and
tons of letters go bundled from the building to all
ends of the earth.

Smiles and tears of each office girl go into the soul of
the building just the same as the master-men who
rule the building.

Hands of clocks turn to noon hours and each floor empties its men and women who go away and eat and come back to work.

Toward the end of the afternoon all work slackens and all jobs go slower as the people feel day closing on them.

One by one the floors are emptied. . . The uniformed elevator men are gone. Pails clang. . . Scrubbers work, talking in foreign tongues. Broom and water and mop clean from the floors human dust and spit, and machine grime of the day.

Spelled in electric fire on the roof are words telling miles of houses and people where to buy a thing for money. The sign speaks till midnight.

Darkness on the hallways. Voices echo. Silence holds. . . Watchmen walk slow from floor to floor and try the doors. Revolvers bulge from their hip pockets. . . Steel safes stand in corners. Money is stacked in them.

A young watchman leans at a window and sees the lights of barges butting their way across a harbor, nets of red and white lanterns in a railroad yard, and a span of glooms splashed with lines of white and blurs of crosses and clusters over the sleeping city.

By night the skyscraper looms in the smoke and the stars and has a soul.

# HANDFULS

# FOG

THE fog comes
on little cat feet.

It sits looking
over harbor and city
on silent haunches
and then moves on.

# POOL

OUT of the fire
Came a man sunken
To less than cinders,
A tea-cup of ashes or so.
And I,
The gold in the house,
Writhed into a stiff pool.

# JAN KUBELIK

Your bow swept over a string, and a long low note
    quivered to the air.
(A mother of Bohemia sobs over a new child perfect
    learning to suck milk.)

Your bow ran fast over all the. high strings fluttering
    and wild.
(All the girls in Bohemia are laughing on a Sunday after-
    noon in the hills with their lovers.)

# CHOOSE

THE single clenched fist lifted and ready,
Or the open asking hand held out and waiting.
Choose :
For we meet by one or the other.

# CRIMSON

Crimson is the slow smolder of the cigar end I hold,
Gray is the ash that stiffens and covers all silent the fire.
(A great man I know is dead and while he lies in his
  coffin a gone flame I sit here in cumbering shadows
  and smoke and watch my thoughts come and go.)

# FLUX

Sand of the sea runs red
Where the sunset reaches and quivers.
Sand of the sea runs yellow
Where the moon slants and wavers.

## KIN

BROTHER, I am fire
Surging under the ocean floor.
I shall never meet you, brother—
Not for years, anyhow;
Maybe thousands of years, brother.
Then I will warm you,
Hold you close, wrap you in circles,
Use you and change you—
Maybe thousands of years, brother.

## WHITE SHOULDERS

Your white shoulders
    I remember
And your shrug of laughter.

    Low laughter
    Shaken slow
From your white shoulders.

## LOSSES

I HAVE love
And a child,
A banjo
And shadows.
(Losses of God,
All will go
And one day
We will hold
Only the shadows.)

# TROTHS

Yellow dust on a bumble
    bee's wing,
Grey lights in a woman's
    asking eyes,
Red ruins in the changing
    sunset embers:
I take you and pile high
    the memories.
Death will break her claws
    on some I keep.

# WAR POEMS
## ( 1914-1915 )

# KILLERS

I AM singing to you
Soft as a man with a dead child speaks;
Hard as a man in handcuffs,
Held where he cannot move:

Under the sun
Are sixteen million men,
Chosen for shining teeth,
Sharp eyes, hard legs,
And a running of young warm blood in their wrists.

And a red juice runs on the green grass;
And a red juice soaks the dark soil.
And the sixteen million are killing . . . and killing
    and killing.

I never forget them day or night:
They beat on my head for memory of them;
They pound on my heart and I cry back to them,
To their homes and women, dreams and games.

I wake in the night and smell the trenches,
And hear the low stir of sleepers in lines—
Sixteen million sleepers and pickets in the dark:
Some of them long sleepers for always,

Some of them tumbling to sleep to-morrow for al-
    ways,
Fixed in the drag of the world's heartbreak,

Eating and drinking, toiling . . . on a long job of
   killing.
Sixteen million men.

# AMONG THE RED GUNS

*After waking at dawn one morning when the wind sang*
*low among dry leaves in an elm*

Among the red guns,
In the hearts of soldiers
Running free blood
In the long, long campaign:
   Dreams go on.

Among the leather saddles,
In the heads of soldiers
Heavy in the wracks and kills
Of all straight fighting:
   Dreams go on.

Among the hot muzzles,
In the hands of soldiers
Brought from flesh-folds of women—
Soft amid the blood and crying—
In all your hearts and heads
Among the guns and saddles and muzzles:

   Dreams,
Dreams go on,
Out of the dead on their backs,
Broken and no use any more:
Dreams of the way and the end go on.

# IRON

Guns,
Long, steel guns,
Pointed from the war ships
In the name of the war god.
Straight, shining, polished guns,
Clambered over with jackies in white blouses,
Glory of tan faces, tousled hair, white teeth,
Laughing lithe jackies in white blouses,
Sitting on the guns singing war songs, war
    chanties.

Shovels,
Broad, iron shovels,
Scooping out oblong vaults,
Loosening turf and leveling sod.

    I ask you
    To witness—
    The shovel is brother to the gun.

# MURMURINGS IN A FIELD HOSPITAL

[*They picked him up in the grass where he had lain two
days in the rain with a piece of shrapnel in his lungs.*]

COME to me only with playthings now . . .
A picture of a singing woman with blue eyes
Standing at a fence of hollyhocks, poppies and sun-
flowers . . .
Or an old man I remember sitting with children telling
stories
Of days that never happened anywhere in the
world . . .

No more iron cold and real to handle,
Shaped for a drive straight ahead.
Bring me only beautiful useless things.
Only old home things touched at sunset in the
quiet . . .
And at the window one day in summer
Yellow of the new crock of butter
Stood against the red of new climbing roses . . .
And the world was all playthings.

## STATISTICS

NAPOLEON shifted,
Restless in the old sarcophagus
And murmured to a watchguard:
" Who goes there? "
" Twenty-one million men,
Soldiers, armies, guns,
Twenty-one million
Afoot, horseback,
In the air,
Under the sea."
And Napoleon turned to his sleep:
" It is not my world answering;
It is some dreamer who knows not
The world I marched in
From Calais to Moscow."
And he slept on
In the old sarcophagus
While the aëroplanes
Droned their motors
Between Napoleon's mausoleum
And the cool night stars.

# FIGHT

RED drips from my chin where I have been eating.
Not all the blood, nowhere near all, is wiped off my
    mouth.

Clots of red mess my hair
And the tiger, the buffalo, know how.

I was a killer.
        Yes, I am a killer.

I come from killing.
        I go to more.
I drive red joy ahead of me from killing.
Red gluts and red hungers run in the smears and juices
    of my inside bones:
The child cries for a suck mother and I cry for war.

# BUTTONS

I HAVE been watching the war map slammed up for
  advertising in front of the newspaper office.
Buttons—red and yellow buttons—blue and black but-
  tons—are shoved back and forth across the map.

A laughing young man, sunny with freckles,
Climbs a ladder, yells a joke to somebody in the crowd,
And then fixes a yellow button one inch west
And follows the yellow button with a black button one
  inch west.

(Ten thousand men and boys twist on their bodies in
  a red soak along a river edge,
Gasping of wounds, calling for water, some rattling
  death in their throats.)
Who would guess what it cost to move two buttons one
  inch on the war map here in front of the newspaper
  office where the freckle-faced young man is laugh-
  ing to us?

# AND THEY OBEY

Smash down the cities.
Knock the walls to pieces.
Break the factories and cathedrals, warehouses
and homes
Into loose piles of stone and lumber and black
burnt wood:
You are the soldiers and we command you.

Build up the cities.
Set up the walls again.
Put together once more the factories and cathe-
drals, warehouses and homes
Into buildings for life and labor:
You are workmen and citizens all: We
command you.

# JAWS

SEVEN nations stood with their hands on the jaws of
   death.
It was the first week in August, Nineteen Hundred Four-
   teen.
I was listening, you were listening, the whole world was
   listening,
And all of us heard a Voice murmuring:
            " I am the way and the light,
            He that believeth on me
            Shall not perish
            But shall have everlasting life."
Seven nations listening heard the Voice and answered:
            " O Hell! "
The jaws of death began clicking and they go on click-
   ing:
            " O Hell! "

# SALVAGE

GUNS on the battle lines have pounded now a year between Brussels and Paris.

And, William Morris, when I read your old chapter on the great arches and naves and little whimsical corners of the Churches of Northern France—Brr-rr!

I'm glad you're a dead man, William Morris, I'm glad you're down in the damp and mouldy, only a memory instead of a living man—I'm glad you're gone.

You never lied to us, William Morris, you loved the shape of those stones piled and carved for you to dream over and wonder because workmen got joy of life into them,

Workmen in aprons singing while they hammered, and praying, and putting their songs and prayers into the walls and roofs, the bastions and cornerstones and gargoyles—all their children and kisses of women and wheat and roses growing.

I say, William Morris, I'm glad you're gone, I'm glad you're a dead man.

Guns on the battle lines have pounded a year now between Brussels and Paris.

# WARS

In the old wars drum of hoofs and the beat of shod feet.
In the new wars hum of motors and the tread of rubber
tires.
In the wars to come silent wheels and whirr of rods not
yet dreamed out in the heads of men.

In the old wars clutches of short swords and jabs into
faces with spears.
In the new wars long range guns and smashed walls, guns
running a spit of metal and men falling in tens and
twenties.
In the wars to come new silent deaths, new silent hurlers
not yet dreamed out in the heads of men.

In the old wars kings quarreling and thousands of men
following.
In the new wars kings quarreling and millions of men
following.
In the wars to come kings kicked under the dust and
millions of men following great causes not yet
dreamed out in the heads of men.

# THE ROAD AND THE END

# THE ROAD AND THE END

I SHALL foot it
Down the roadway in the dusk,
Where shapes of hunger wander
And the fugitives of pain go by.
I shall foot it
In the silence of the morning,
See the night slur into dawn,
Hear the slow great winds arise
Where tall trees flank the way
And shoulder toward the sky.

The broken boulders by the road
Shall not commemorate my ruin.
Regret shall be the gravel under foot.
I shall watch for
Slim birds swift of wing
That go where wind and ranks of thunder
Drive the wild processionals of rain.

The dust of the traveled road
Shall touch my hands and face.

# CHOICES

THEY offer you many things,
    I a few.
Moonlight on the play of fountains at night
With water sparkling a drowsy monotone,
Bare-shouldered, smiling women and talk
And a cross-play of loves and adulteries
And a fear of death
              and a remembering of regrets:
All this they offer you.
I come with:
    salt and bread
    a terrible job of work
    and tireless war;
Come and have now:
    hunger.
    danger
    and hate.

# GRAVES

I DREAMED one man stood against a thousand,
One man damned as a wrongheaded fool.
One year and another he walked the streets,
And a thousand shrugs and hoots
Met him in the shoulders and mouths he passed.

He died alone
And only the undertaker came to his funeral.

Flowers grow over his grave anod in the wind,
And over the graves of the thousand, too,
The flowers grow anod in the wind.

Flowers and the wind,
Flowers anod over the graves of the dead,
Petals of red, leaves of yellow, streaks of white,
Masses of purple sagging . . .
I love you and your great way of forgetting.

# AZTEC MASK

I WANTED a man's face looking into the jaws and throat
    of life
With something proud on his face, so proud no smash
    of the jaws,
No gulp of the throat leaves the face in the end
With anything else than the old proud look:
        Even to the finish, dumped in the dust,
        Lost among the used-up cinders,
        This face, men would say, is a flash,
        Is laid on bones taken from the ribs of the earth,
        Ready for the hammers of changing, changing
           years,
        Ready for the sleeping, sleeping years of silence.
        Ready for the dust and fire and wind.
I wanted this face and I saw it today in an Aztec mask.
A cry out of storm and dark, a red yell and a purple
    prayer,
A beaten shape of ashes
        waiting the sunrise or night,
        something or nothing,
        proud-mouthed,
        proud-eyed gambler.

# MOMUS

Momus is the name men give your face,
The brag of its tone, like a long low steamboat whistle
Finding a way mid mist on a shoreland,
Where gray rocks let the salt water shatter spray
  Against horizons purple, silent.


  Yes, Momus,
Men have flung your face in bronze
To gaze in gargoyle downward on a street-whirl of folk.
They were artists did this, shaped your sad mouth,
Gave you a tall forehead slanted with calm, broad wis-
    dom;
All your lips to the corners and your cheeks to the high
    bones
Thrown over and through with a smile that forever
    wishes and wishes, purple, silent, fled from all the
    iron things of life, evaded like a sought bandit, gone
    into dreams, by God.


I wonder, Momus,
Whether shadows of the dead sit somewhere and look
    with deep laughter
On men who play in terrible earnest the old, known,
    solemn repetitions of history.


A droning monotone soft as sea laughter hovers from
    your kindliness of bronze,
You give me the human ease of a mountain peak, purple,
    silent;
Granite shoulders heaving above the earth curves,

Careless eye-witness of the spawning tides of men and
    women
Swarming always in a drift of millions to the dust of toil,
    the salt of tears,
And blood drops of undiminishing war.

# THE ANSWER

You have spoken the answer.
A child searches far sometimes
Into the red dust
            On a dark rose leaf
And so you have gone far
            For the answer is:
                        Silence.


   In the republic
Of the winking stars
            and spent cataclysms
Sure we are it is off there the answer
      is hidden and folded over,
Sleeping in the sun, careless whether
      it is Sunday or any other day of
      the week,


Knowing silence will bring all one way
      or another.


Have we not seen
Purple of the pansy
            out of the mulch
            and mold
            crawl
            into a dusk
            of velvet?
            blur of yellow?

Almost we thought from nowhere but it was
     the silence,
               the future,
               working.

# TO A DEAD MAN

Over the dead line we have called to you
To come across with a word to us,
Some beaten whisper of what happens
Where you are over the dead line
Deaf to our calls and voiceless.

The flickering shadows have not answered
Nor your lips sent a signal
Whether love talks and roses grow
And the sun breaks at morning
Splattering the sea with crimson.

# UNDER

I AM the undertow
Washing tides of power
Battering the pillars
Under your things of high law.

I am a sleepless
Slowfaring eater,
Maker of rust and rot
In your bastioned fastenings,
Caissons deep.

I am the Law
Older than you
And your builders proud.

I am deaf
In all days
Whether you
Say " Yes " or " No ".

I am the crumbler:
   To-morrow.

# A SPHINX

CLOSE-MOUTHED you sat five thousand years and never
    let out a whisper.

Processions came by, marchers, asking questions you
    answered with grey eyes never blinking, shut lips
    never talking.

Not one croak of anything you know has come from your
    cat crouch of ages.

I am one of those who know all you know and I keep my
    questions:  I know the answers you hold.

# WHO AM I?

My head knocks against the stars.

My feet are on the hilltops.

My finger-tips are in the valleys and shores of
universal life.

Down in the sounding foam of primal things I
reach my hands and play with pebbles of
destiny.

I have been to hell and back many times.

I know all about heaven, for I have talked with
God.

I dabble in the blood and guts of the terrible.

I know the passionate seizure of beauty

And the marvelous rebellion of man at all signs
reading " Keep Off."

My name is Truth and I am the most elusive cap-
tive in the universe.

## OUR PRAYER OF THANKS

FOR the gladness here where the sun is shining at even-
      ing on the weeds at the river,
   Our prayer of thanks.

For the laughter of children who tumble barefooted and
      bareheaded in the summer grass,
   Our prayer of thanks.

For the sunset and the stars, the women and the white
      arms that hold us,
   Our prayer of thanks.

   God,
If you are deaf and blind, if this is all lost to you,
God, if the dead in their coffins amid the silver handles
      on the edge of town, or the reckless dead of war
      days thrown unknown in pits, if these dead are for-
      ever deaf and blind and lost,
   Our prayer of thanks.

   God,
The game is all your way, the secrets and the signals and
      the system; and so for the break of the game and
      the first play and the last.
   Our prayer of thanks.

# FOGS AND FIRES

# AT A WINDOW

GIVE me hunger,
O you gods that sit and give
The world its orders.
Give me hunger, pain and want,
Shut me out with shame and failure
From your doors of gold and fame,
Give me your shabbiest, weariest hunger!

But leave me a little love,
A voice to speak to me in the day end,
A hand to touch me in the dark room
Breaking the long loneliness.
In the dusk of day-shapes
Blurring the sunset,
One little wandering, western star
Thrust out from the changing shores of shadow.
Let me go to the window,
Watch there the day-shapes of dusk
And wait and know the coming
Of a little love.

# UNDER THE HARVEST MOON

Under the harvest moon,
When the soft silver
Drips shimmering
Over the garden nights,
Death, the gray mocker,
Comes and whispers to you
As a beautiful friend
Who remembers.

Under the summer roses
When the flagrant crimson
Lurks in the dusk
Of the wild red leaves,
Love, with little hands,
Comes and touches you
With a thousand memories,
And asks you
Beautiful, unanswerable questions.

# THE GREAT HUNT

I CANNOT tell you now;
    When the wind's drive and whirl
    Blow me along no longer,
    And the wind's a whisper at last—
Maybe I'll tell you then—
                      some other time.

    When the rose's flash to the sunset
    Reels to the rack and the twist,
    And the rose is a red bygone,
    When the face I love is going
    And the gate to the end shall clang,
    And it's no use to beckon or say, " So long "—
Maybe I'll tell you then—
                      some other time.

I never knew any more beautiful than you:
    I have hunted you under my thoughts,
    I have broken down under the wind
    And into the roses looking for you.
      I shall never find any
                  greater than you.

# MONOTONE

THE monotone of the rain is beautiful,
And the sudden rise and slow relapse
Of the long multitudinous rain.

The sun on the hills is beautiful,
Or a captured sunset sea-flung,
Bannered with fire and gold.

A face I know is beautiful—
With fire and gold of sky and sea,
And the peace of long warm rain.

# JOY

LET a joy keep you.
Reach out your hands
And take it when it runs by,
As the Apache dancer
Clutches his woman.
I have seen them
Live long and laugh loud,
Sent on singing, singing,
Smashed to the heart
Under the ribs
With a terrible love.
Joy always,
Joy everywhere—
Let joy kill you!
Keep away from the little deaths.

# SHIRT

I REMEMBER once I ran after you and tagged the flutter-
  ing shirt of you in the wind.
Once many days ago I drank a glassful of something and
  the picture of you shivered and slid on top of the
  stuff.
And again it was nobody else but you I heard in the
  singing voice of a careless humming woman.
One night when I sat with chums telling stories at a
  bonfire flickering red embers, in a language its own
  talking to a spread of white stars:
        It was you that slunk laughing
        in the clumsy staggering shadows.
Broken answers of remembrance let me know you are
  alive with a peering phantom face behind a doorway
  somewhere in the city's push and fury
Or under a pack of moss and leaves waiting in silence
  under a twist of oaken arms ready as ever to run
  away again when I tag the fluttering shirt of you.

# AZTEC

You came from the Aztecs
With a copper on your fore-arms
Tawnier than a sunset
Saying good-by to an even river.

And I said, you remember,
Those fore-arms of yours
Were finer than bronzes
And you were glad.

                    It was tears
And a path west
                    and a home-going
                    when I asked
Why there were scars of worn gold
Where a man's ring was fixed once
On your third finger.
                    And I call you
To come back
                    before the days are longer.

## TWO

Memory of you is . . . a blue spear of flower.
I cannot remember the name of it.
Alongside a bold dripping poppy is fire and silk.
                              And they cover you.

# BACK YARD

SHINE on, O moon of summer.
Shine to the leaves of grass, catalpa and oak,
All silver under your rain to-night.

An Italian boy is sending songs to you to-night from an
    accordion.
A Polish boy is out with his best girl; they marry next
    month; to-night they are throwing you kisses.

An old man next door is dreaming over a sheen that sits
    in a cherry tree in his back yard.

The clocks say I must go—I stay here sitting on the
    back porch drinking white thoughts you rain down.

    Shine on, O moon,
Shake out more and more silver changes.

## ON THE BREAKWATER

On the breakwater in the summer dark, a man and a
    girl are sitting,
She across his knee and they are looking face into face
Talking to each other without words, singing rythms in
    silence to each other.

A funnel of white ranges the blue dusk from an out-
    going boat,
Playing its searchlight, puzzled, abrupt, over a streak of
    green,
And two on the breakwater keep their silence, she on his
    knee.

# MASK

FLING your red scarf faster and faster, dancer.
It is summer and the sun loves a million green leaves,
    masses of green.
Your red scarf flashes across them calling and a-calling.
The silk and flare of it is a great soprano leading a
    chorus
Carried along in a rouse of voices reaching for the heart
    of the world.
Your toes are singing to meet the song of your arms:

Let the red scarf go swifter.
Summer and the sun command you.

# PEARL FOG

Open the door now.
Go roll up the collar of your coat
To walk in the changing scarf of mist.

Tell your sins here to the pearl fog
And know for once a deepening night
Strange as the half-meanings
Alurk in a wise woman's mousey eyes.

Yes, tell your sins
And know how careless a pearl fog is
Of the laws you have broken.

# I SANG

I SANG to you and the moon
But only the moon remembers.
  I sang
O reckless free-hearted
               free-throated rythms,
Even the moon remembers them
  And is kind to me.

# FOLLIES

Shaken,
The blossoms of lilac,
  And shattered,
The atoms of purple.
Green dip the leaves,
  Darker the bark,
Longer the shadows.

Sheer lines of poplar
Shimmer with masses of silver
And down in a garden old with years
And broken walls of ruin and story,
Roses rise with red rain-memories.
        May!
  In the open world
The sun comes and finds your face,
  Remembering all.

# JUNE

PAULA is digging and shaping the loam of a salvia,
  Scarlet Chinese talker of summer.
Two petals of crabapple blossom blow fallen in Paula's
    hair,
  And fluff of white from a cottonwood.

## NOCTURNE IN A DESERTED
## BRICKYARD

STUFF of the moon
Runs on the lapping sand
Out to the longest shadows.
Under the curving willows,
And round the creep of the wave line,
Fluxions of yellow and dusk on the waters
Make a wide dreaming pansy of an old pond in the night.

# HYDRANGEAS

DRAGOONS, I tell you the white hydrangeas
    turn rust and go soon.
Already mid September a line of brown runs
    over them.
One sunset after another tracks the faces, the
    petals.
Waiting, they look over the fence for what
    way they go.

## THEME IN YELLOW

I SPOT the hills
With yellow balls in autumn.
I light the prairie cornfields
Orange and tawny gold clusters
And I am called pumpkins.
On the last of October
When dusk is fallen
Children join hands
And circle round me
Singing ghost songs
And love to the harvest moon;
I am a jack-o'-lantern
With terrible teeth
And the children know
I am fooling.

# BETWEEN TWO HILLS

BETWEEN two hills
The old town stands.
The houses loom
And the roofs and trees
And the dusk and the dark,
The damp and the dew
    Are there.

The prayers are said
And the people rest
For sleep is there
And the touch of dreams
    Is over all.

# LAST ANSWERS

I WROTE a poem on the mist
And a woman asked me what I meant by it.
I had thought till then only of the beauty of the mist,
    how pearl and gray of it mix and reel,
And change the drab shanties with lighted lamps at even-
    ing into points of mystery quivering with color.

   I answered:
The whole world was mist once long ago and some day
    it will all go back to mist,
Our skulls and lungs are more water than bone and
    tissue
And all poets love dust and mist because all the last
    answers
Go running back to dust and mist.

# WINDOW

NIGHT from a railroad car window
Is a great, dark, soft thing
Broken across with slashes of light.

# YOUNG SEA

THE sea is never still.
It pounds on the shore
Restless as a young heart,
Hunting.

The sea speaks
And only the stormy hearts
Know what it says:
It is the face
        of a rough mother speaking.

The sea is young.
One storm cleans all the hoar
And loosens the age of it.
I hear it laughing, reckless.

They love the sea,
Men who ride on it
And know they will die
Under the salt of it

Let only the young come,
    Says the sea.

Let them kiss my face
    And hear me.

I am the last word
  And I tell
Where storms and stars come from.

# BONES

SLING me under the sea.
Pack me down in the salt and wet.
No farmer's plow shall touch my bones.
No Hamlet hold my jaws and speak
How jokes are gone and empty is my mouth.
Long, green-eyed scavengers shall pick my eyes,
Purple fish play hide-and-seek,
And I shall be song of thunder, crash of sea,
Down on the floors of salt and wet.
        Sling me . . . under the sea.

# PALS

TAKE a hold now
On the silver handles here,
Six silver handles,
One for each of his old pals.

Take hold
And lift him down the stairs,
Put him on the rollers
Over the floor of the hearse.

Take him on the last haul,
To the cold straight house,
The level even house,
To the last house of all.

   The dead say nothing
   And the dead know much
   And the dead hold under their tongues
   A locked-up story.

# CHILD

THE young child, Christ, is straight and wise
And asks questions of the old men, questions
Found under running water for all children
And found under shadows thrown on still waters
By tall trees looking downward, old and gnarled.
Found to the eyes of children alone, untold,
Singing a low song in the loneliness.
And the young child, Christ, goes on asking
And the old men answer nothing and only know love
For the young child. Christ, straight and wise.

# POPPIES

SHE loves blood-red poppies for a garden to walk in.
In a loose white gown she walks
                 and a new child tugs at cords in her body.
Her head to the west at evening when the dew is creep-
    ing,
A shudder of gladness runs in her bones and torsal fiber:
She loves blood-red poppies for a garden to walk in.

# CHILD MOON

THE child's wonder
At the old moon
Comes back nightly.
She points her finger
To the far silent yellow thing
Shining through the branches
Filtering on the leaves a golden sand,
Crying with her little tongue, " See the moon! "
And in her bed fading to sleep
With babblings of the moon on her little mouth.

# MARGARET

Many birds and the beating of wings
Make a flinging reckless hum
In the early morning at the rocks
Above the blue pool
Where the gray shadows swim lazy.

In your blue eyes, O reckless child,
I saw today many little wild wishes,
Eager as the great morning.

# SHADOWS

# POEMS DONE ON A LATE NIGHT CAR

I AM The Great White Way of the city:
When you ask what is my desire, I answer:
" Girls fresh as country wild flowers,
With young faces tired of the cows and barns,
Eager in their eyes as the dawn to find my mysteries,
Slender supple girls with shapely legs,
Lure in the arch of their little shoulders
And wisdom from the prairies to cry only softly at
    the ashes of my mysteries."

*Lines based on certain regrets that come with rumina-*
*tion upon the painted faces of women on*
*North Clark Street, Chicago*

Roses,
Red roses,
Crushed
In the rain and wind
Like mouths of women
Beaten by the fists of
Men using them.
 O little roses
 And broken leaves
 And petal wisps :
You that so flung your crimson
 To the sun
Only yesterday.

### III.  HOME

Here is a thing my heart wishes the world had more of:
I heard it in the air of one night when I listened
To a mother singing softly to a child restless and angry
    in the darkness.

# IT IS MUCH

WOMEN of night life amid the lights
Where the line of your full, round throats
Matches in gleam the glint of your eyes
And the ring of your heart-deep laughter:
  It is much to be warm and sure of to-morrow.

Women of night life along the shadows,
Lean at your throats and skulking the walls,
Gaunt as a bitch worn to the bone,
Under the paint of your smiling faces:
  It is much to be warm and sure of to-morrow.

# TRAFFICKER

AMONG the shadows where two streets cross,
A woman lurks in the dark and waits
To move on when a policeman heaves in view.
Smiling a broken smile from a face
Painted over haggard bones and desperate eyes,
All night she offers passers-by what they will
Of her beauty wasted, body faded, claims gone,
And no takers.

# HARRISON STREET COURT

I HEARD a woman's lips
Speaking to a companion
Say these words:

" A woman what hustles
Never keeps nothin'
For all her hustlin'.
Somebody always gets
What she goes on the street for.
If it ain't a pimp
It's a bull what gets it.
I been hustlin' now
Till I ain't much good any more.
I got nothin' to show for it.
Some man got it all,
Every night's hustlin' I ever did."

# SOILED DOVE

LET us be honest; the lady was not a harlot until she
married a corporation lawyer who picked her from
a Ziegfeld chorus.

Before then she never took anybody's money and paid
for her silk stockings out of what she earned singing
and dancing.

She loved one man and he loved six women and the
game was changing her looks, calling for more and
more massage money and high coin for the beauty
doctors.

Now she drives a long, underslung motor car all by her-
self, reads in the day's papers what her husband is
doing to the inter-state commerce commission, re-
quires a larger corsage from year to year, and won-
ders sometimes how one man is coming along with
six women.

# JUNGHEIMER'S

In western fields of corn and northern timber lands,
  They talk about me, a saloon with a soul,
  The soft red lights, the long curving bar,
  The leather seats and dim corners,
  Tall brass spittoons, a nigger cutting ham,
And the painting of a woman half-dressed thrown reck-
  less across a bed after a night of booze and riots.

# GONE

EVERYBODY loved Chick Lorimer in our town.
                    Far off
            Everybody loved her.
So we all love a wild girl keeping a hold
            On a dream she wants.
Nobody knows now where Chick Lorimer went.
Nobody knows why she packed her trunk . . a few
    old things
And is gone,
                    Gone with her little chin
                    Thrust ahead of her
                    And her soft hair blowing careless
                    From under a wide hat,
Dancer, singer, a laughing passionate lover.

Were there ten men or a hundred hunting Chick?
Were there five men or fifty with aching hearts?
            Everybody loved Chick Lorimer.
                Nobody knows where she's gone.

# OTHER DAYS
## ( 1900-1910 )

# DREAMS IN THE DUSK

DREAMS in the dusk,
Only dreams closing the day
And with the day's close going back
To the gray things, the dark things,
The far, deep things of dreamland.

Dreams, only dreams in the dusk,
Only the old remembered pictures
Of lost days when the day's loss
Wrote in tears the heart's loss.

Tears and loss and broken dreams
May find your heart at dusk.

# DOCKS

Strolling along
By the teeming docks,
I watch the ships put out.
Black ships that heave and lunge
And move like mastodons
Arising from lethargic sleep.

The fathomed harbor
Calls them not nor dares
Them to a strain of action,
But outward, on and outward,
Sounding low-reverberating calls,
Shaggy in the half-lit distance,
They pass the pointed headland,
View the wide, far-lifting wilderness
And leap with cumulative speed
To test the challenge of the sea.

Plunging,
Doggedly onward plunging,
Into salt and mist and foam and sun.

# ALL DAY LONG

ALL day long in fog and wind,
The waves have flung their beating crests
Against the palisades of adamant.
    My boy, he went to sea, long and long ago,
    Curls of brown were slipping underneath his cap,
    He looked at me from blue and steely eyes;
    Natty, straight and true, he stepped away,
    My boy, he went to sea.
All day long in fog and wind,
The waves have flung their beating crests
Against the palisades of adamant.

# WAITING

TODAY I will let the old boat stand
Where the sweep of the harbor tide comes in
To the pulse of a far, deep-steady sway.
And I will rest and dream and sit on the deck
    Watching the world go by
And take my pay for many hard days gone I re-
member.

I will choose what clouds I like
In the great white fleets that wander the blue
As I lie on my back or loaf at the rail.
And I will listen as the veering winds kiss me and
    fold me
And put on my brow the touch of the world's great
    will.

Daybreak will hear the heart of the boat beat,
    Engine throb and piston play
In the quiver and leap at call of life.
To-morrow we move in the gaps and heights
On changing floors of unlevel seas
And no man shall stop us and no man follow
For ours is the quest of an unknown shore
And we are husky and lusty and shouting-gay.

# FROM THE SHORE

A LONE gray bird,
Dim-dipping, far-flying,
Alone in the shadows and grandeurs and tumults
Of night and the sea
And the stars and storms.

Out over the darkness it wavers and hovers,
Out into the gloom it swings and batters,
Out into the wind and the rain and the vast,
Out into the pit of a great black world,
Where fogs are at battle, sky-driven, sea-blown,
Love of mist and rapture of flight,
Glories of chance and hazards of death
On its eager and palpitant wings.

Out into the deep of the great dark world,
Beyond the long borders where foam and drift
Of the sundering waves are lost and gone
On the tides that plunge and rear and crumble.

# UPLANDS IN MAY

Wonder as of old things
Fresh and fair come back
Hangs over pasture and road.
Lush in the lowland grasses rise
And upland beckons to upland.
The great strong hills are humble.

# DREAM GIRL

You will come one day in a waver of love,
Tender as dew, impetuous as rain,
The tan of the sun will be on your skin,
The purr of the breeze in your murmuring speech,
You will pose with a hill-flower grace.

You will come, with your slim, expressive arms,
A poise of the head no sculptor has caught
And nuances spoken with shoulder and neck,
Your face in a pass-and-repass of moods
As many as skies in delicate change
Of cloud and blue and flimmering sun.

                    Yet,
You may not come, O girl of a dream,
We may but pass as the world goes by
And take from a look of eyes into eyes,
A film of hope and a memoried day.

# PLOWBOY

AFTER the last red sunset glimmer,
Black on the line of a low hill rise,
Formed into moving shadows, I saw
A plowboy and two horses lined against the
    gray,
Plowing in the dusk the last furrow.
The turf had a gleam of brown,
And smell of soil was in the air,
And, cool and moist, a haze of April.

I shall remember you long,
Plowboy and horses against the sky in shadow.
I shall remember you and the picture
You made for me,
Turning the turf in the dusk
And haze of an April gloaming.

# BROADWAY

I SHALL never forget you, Broadway
Your golden and calling lights.

I'll remember you long,
Tall-walled river of rush and play.

Hearts that know you hate you
And lips that have given you laughter
Have gone to their ashes of life and its roses,
Cursing the dreams that were lost
In the dust of your harsh and trampled stones.

## OLD WOMAN

THE owl-car clatters along, dogged by the echo
From building and battered paving-stone;
The headlight scoffs at the mist
And fixes its yellow rays in the cold slow rain;
Against a pane I press my forehead
And drowsily look on the walls and sidewalks.

The headlight finds the way
And life is gone from the wet and the welter—
Only an old woman, bloated, disheveled and bleared.
Far-wandered waif of other days,
Huddles for sleep in a doorway,
Homeless.

# NOON HOUR

SHE sits in the dust at the walls
  And makes cigars,
Bending at the bench
With fingers wage-anxious,
Changing her sweat for the day's pay.

Now the noon hour has come,
And she leans with her bare arms
On the window-sill over the river,
Leans and feels at her throat
Cool-moving things out of the free open ways:

At her throat and eyes and nostrils
The touch and the blowing cool
Of great free ways beyond the walls.

# 'BOES

I WAITED today for a freight train to pass.

Cattle cars with steers butting their horns against the
bars, went by.

And a half a dozen hoboes stood on bumpers between
cars.

Well, the cattle are respectable, I thought.

Every steer has its transportation paid for by the farmer
sending it to market,

While the hoboes are law-breakers in riding a railroad
train without a ticket.

It reminded me of ten days I spent in the Allegheny
County jail in Pittsburgh.

I got ten days even though I was a veteran of the Span-
ish-American war.

Cooped in the same cell with me was an old man, a
bricklayer and a booze-fighter.

But it just happened he, too, was a veteran soldier, and
he had fought to preserve the Union and free the
niggers.

We were three in all, the other being a Lithuanian who
got drunk on pay day at the steel works and got to
fighting a policeman;

All the clothes he had was a shirt, pants and shoes—
somebody got his hat and coat and what money he
had left over when he got drunk.

# UNDER A TELEPHONE POLE

I AM a copper wire slung in the air,
Slim against the sun I make not even a clear line of
    shadow.
Night and day I keep singing—humming and thrum-
    ming:
It is love and war and money; it is the fighting and the
    tears, the work and want,
Death and laughter of men and women passing through
    me, carrier of your speech,
In the rain and the wet dripping, in the dawn and the
    shine drying,
        A copper wire.

# I AM THE PEOPLE, THE MOB

I AM the people—the mob—the crowd—the mass.

Do you know that all the great work of the world is done through me?

I am the workingman, the inventor, the maker of the world's food and clothes.

I am the audience that witnesses history. The Napoleons come from me and the Lincolns. They die. And then I send forth more Napoleons and Lincolns.

I am the seed ground. I am a prairie that will stand for much plowing. Terrible storms pass over me. I forget. The best of me is sucked out and wasted. I forget. Everything but Death comes to me and makes me work and give up what I have. And I forget.

Sometimes I growl, shake myself and spatter a few red drops for history to remember. Then—I forget.

When I, the People, learn to remember, when I, the People, use the lessons of yesterday and no longer forget who robbed me last year, who played me for a fool—then there will be no speaker in all the world say the name: "The People," with any fleck of a sneer in his voice or any far-off smile of derision.

The mob—the crowd—the mass—will arrive then.

# GOVERNMENT

THE Government—I heard about the Government and I went out to find it. I said I would look closely at it when I saw it.

Then I saw a policeman dragging a drunken man to the callaboose. It was the Government in action.

I saw a ward alderman slip into an office one morning and talk with a judge. Later in the day the judge dismissed a case against a pickpocket who was a live ward worker for the alderman. Again I saw this was the Government, doing things.

I saw militiamen level their rifles at a crowd of workingmen who were trying to get other workingmen to stay away from a shop where there was a strike on. Government in action.

Everywhere I saw that Government is a thing made of men, that Government has blood and bones, it is many mouths whispering into many ears, sending telegrams, aiming rifles, writing orders, saying " yes " and " no."

Government dies as the men who form it die and are laid away in their graves and the new Government that comes after is human, made of heartbeats of blood, ambitions, lusts, and money running through it all, money paid and money taken, and money covered up and spoken of with hushed voices.

A Government is just as secret and mysterious and sensitive as any human sinner carrying a load of germs, traditions and corpuscles handed down from fathers and mothers away back.

# LANGUAGES

THERE are no handles upon a language
Whereby men take hold of it
And mark it with signs for its remembrance.
It is a river, this language,
Once in a thousand years
Breaking a new course
Changing its way to the ocean.
It is mountain effluvia
Moving to valleys
And from nation to nation
Crossing borders and mixing.
Languages die like rivers.
Words wrapped round your tongue today
And broken to shape of thought
Between your teeth and lips speaking
Now and today
Shall be faded hieroglyphics
Ten thousand years from now.
Sing—and singing—remember
Your song dies and changes
And is not here to-morrow
Any more than the wind
Blowing ten thousand years ago.

# LETTERS TO DEAD IMAGISTS

EMILY DICKINSON:
You gave us the bumble bee who has a soul,
The everlasting traveler among the hollyhocks,
And how God plays around a back yard garden.

STEVIE CRANE:
War is kind and we never knew the kindness of war till
  you came;
Nor the black riders and clashes of spear and shield out
  of the sea,
Nor the mumblings and shots that rise from dreams on
  call.

# SHEEP

Thousands of sheep, soft-footed, black-nosed sheep—
one by one going up the hill and over the fence—one by
one four-footed pattering up and over—one by one wig-
gling their stub tails as they take the short jump and go
over—one by one silently unless for the multitudinous
drumming of their hoofs as they move on and go over—
thousands and thousands of them in the grey haze of
evening just after sundown—one by one slanting in a
long line to pass over the hill—

I am the slow, long-legged Sleepyman and I love you
sheep in Persia, California, Argentine, Australia, or
Spain—you are the thoughts that help me when I, the
Sleepyman, lay my hands on the eyelids of the children
of the world at eight o'clock every night—you thousands
and thousands of sheep in a procession of dusk making
an endless multitudinous drumming on the hills with
your hoofs.

# THE RED SON

I LOVE your faces I saw the many years
I drank your milk and filled my mouth
With your home talk, slept in your house
And was one of you.
                              But a fire burns in my heart.
Under the ribs where pulses thud
And flitting between bones of skull
Is the push, the endless mysterious command,
                    Saying:
" I leave you behind—
You for the little hills and the years all alike,
You with your patient cows and old houses
Protected from the rain,
I am going away and I never come back to you;
Crags and high rough places call me,
Great places of death
Where men go empty handed
And pass over smiling
To the star-drift on the horizon rim.
My last whisper shall be alone, unknown;
I shall go to the city and fight against it,
And make it give me passwords
Of luck and love, women worth dying for,
And  money.
                    I go where you wist not of
                    Nor I nor any man nor woman.
                    I only know I go to storms
                    Grappling against things wet and naked."

There is no pity of it and no blame.
None of us is in the wrong.
After all it is only this:
        You for the little hills and I go away.

# THE MIST

I AM the mist, the impalpable mist,
Back of the thing you seek.
My arms are long,
Long as the reach of time and space.

Some toil and toil, believing,
Looking now and again on my face,
Catching a vital, olden glory.

But no one passes me,
I tangle and snare them all.
I am the cause of the Sphinx,
The voiceless, baffled, patient Sphinx.

I was at the first of things,
I will be at the last.
        I am the primal mist
        And no man passes me;
        My long impalpable arms
        Bar them all.

# THE JUNK MAN

I AM glad God saw Death
And gave Death a job taking care of all who are tired
    of living:

When all the wheels in a clock are worn and slow and
    the connections loose
And the clock goes on ticking and telling the wrong time
    from hour to hour
And people around the house joke about what a bum
    clock it is,
How glad the clock is when the big Junk Man drives
    his wagon
Up to the house and puts his arms around the clock and
    says:
        "You don't belong here,
        You gotta come
        Along with me,"
How glad the clock is then, when it feels the arms of the
    Junk Man close around it and carry it away.

# SILVER NAILS

A MAN was crucified. He came to the city a stranger, was accused, and nailed to a cross. He lingered hanging. Laughed at the crowd. " The nails are iron," he said, " You are cheap. In my country when we crucify we use silver nails . . ." So he went jeering. They did not understand him at first. Later they talked about him in changed voices in the saloons, bowling alleys, and churches. It came over them every man is crucified only once in his life and the law of humanity dictates silver nails be used for the job. A statue was erected to him in a public square. Not having gathered his name when he was among them, they wrote him as John Silvernail on the statue.

# GYPSY

I ASKED a gypsy pal
To imitate an old image
And speak old wisdom.
She drew in her chin,
Made her neck and head
The top piece of a Nile obelisk
    and said:
Snatch off the gag from thy mouth, child,
And be free to keep silence.
Tell no man anything for no man listens,
Yet hold thy lips ready to speak.

# PRAIRIE STATE BOOKS